The Organic Guide *to* Edible Gardens

The Organic Guide *to* Edible Gardens

Jennifer Stackhouse & Debbie McDonald

MURDOCH BOOKS

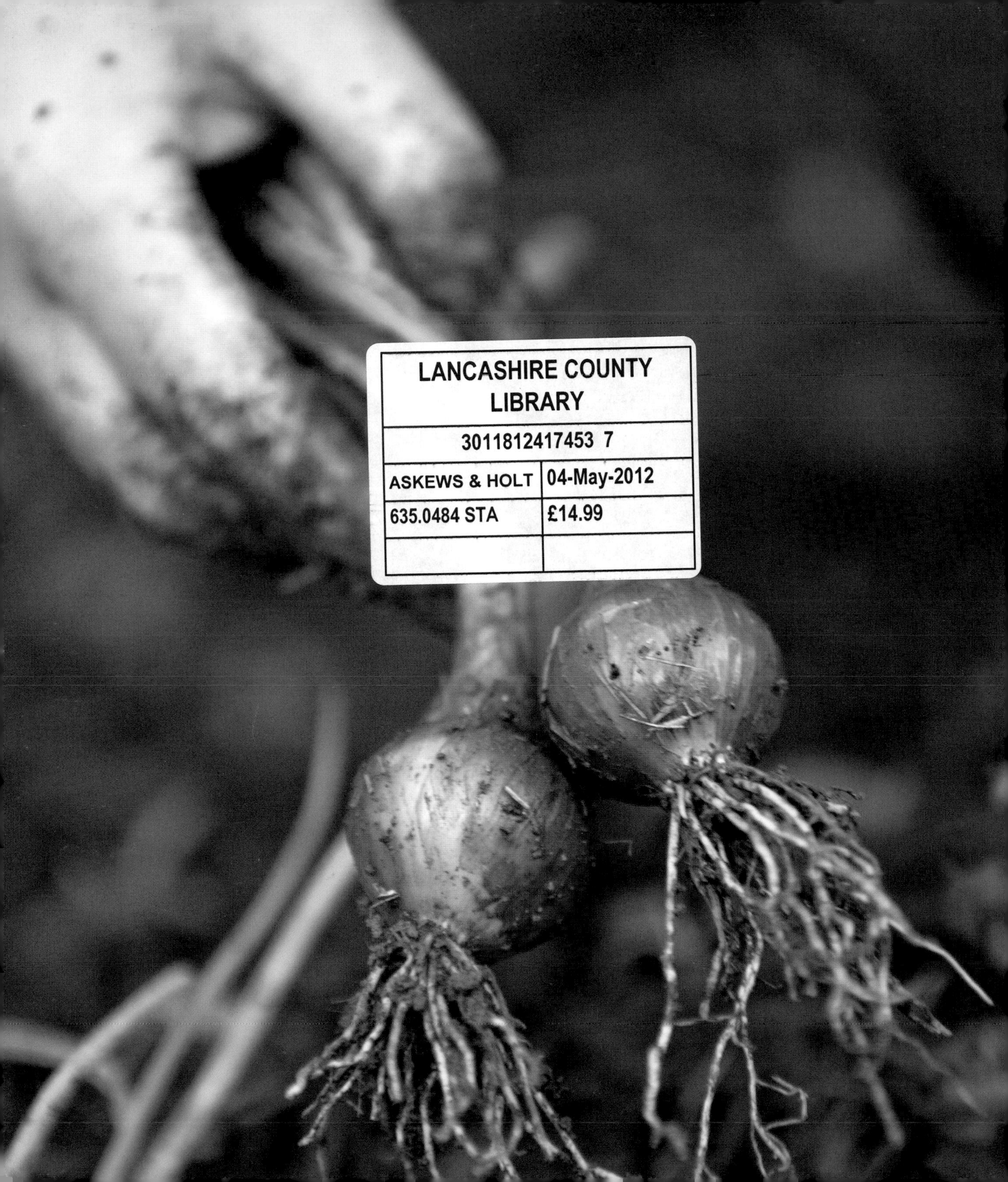

Contents

Welcome

Jennifer Stackhouse

Don't worry if you don't have a hemp shirt, a mud brick house that you've built yourself or a bicycle. You can live a modern life and still be an organic gardener. Organic principles work whether you are living in the inner city, the suburbs or you've found a rural hideaway.

It is safe to say that Debbie McDonald and I are both passionate gardeners who love talking and writing about plants, gardens and the things that make them tick. We both have gardens—not show places but working gardens. My garden is set on a rural block of just over two hectares on the outskirts of Sydney while Debbie has more of a city garden that she enjoys tending with her young daughter.

We trace our love of gardens to our families and particularly to our mothers and grandmothers who were all keen gardeners.

But it doesn't stop there. Debbie and I work together on ABC *Gardening Australia* magazine so working together on this book—the first in a series of practical garden guides—seemed like a natural progression.

While Debbie set out, tools in hand, with photographer Ian Hofstetter, to create many of the photographs that are found throughout these pages, I was sitting diligently at the computer putting together the words. Well perhaps not too diligently as I find it very hard not to be distracted by what's happening outside in my garden, over at the chook shed or with the horses in the paddocks that surround the house. A wilting plant may catch my eye or an overflowing bucket of scraps that just has to be taken to the chooks.

Of course once I've found that excuse to head out the door, it is very easy not to go back inside. There are always weeds to be pulled out, crops to be picked and plants to be watered. I like to watch the insects at work among my plants and stop and listen to the parrots squabbling in the trees. But that's the joy of a garden—it's a work in progress and it's your domain.

This book is our attempt to share the joy we derive from our gardens with you. We think gardening should be fun, rewarding and environmentally friendly. Sure it can be hard work. Sometimes you get hot and tired and mostly you get dirty but, at the end of time spent in your garden, you have the satisfaction of feeling that you've done something towards creating an oasis in what's fast becoming a very big, bustling and busy world.

Gardens don't have to be grand and they don't have to cost lots of money to create. We think that anyone, anywhere can experience the joy of gardening and particularly of productive gardening.

With all this in mind we have put together a book that will help you in the garden much like a friend who is there to offer advice over the back fence. We don't want to get bogged down in too many rules or make organic gardening seem too hard to combine with everyday life. So you may say this is organic 'lite', but there's still plenty of stuff to get your teeth into.

This book is designed for gardeners who want to take an organic approach to growing plants—particularly productive plants. We've outlined the basics, offered some advice to help you to better understand your plants and some tips on how to manage your garden day by day. Importantly we've tried to put it together so that it is easy to read and easy to understand.

Inside the book are chapters on planning your garden, making compost and dealing with pests and diseases in a manner that's both effective and safe.

We've also tackled the question of just what the term organic means. For us it is about taking a holistic approach to your garden by seeing the garden as part of an integrated system that you control and work within. It is also about looking back and learning from gardening as practised by our grandparents who didn't rely on prepared solutions for feeding or pest and disease control.

Debbie McDonald

If you want to start a productive organic garden from scratch or just adapt your existing garden this book provides all the help and guidance you need. Then, to manage your garden from day to day, you can refer to the chapters on maintenance or pests and diseases. For a quick find, head to the index at the back of the book. Just before the index you will find further reading, useful websites and other helpful resources.

We hope this book helps you create the garden you want and leads you to develop a life-long joy of your outdoors.

Happy organic gardening!

Jennifer Stackhouse and Debbie McDonald

CHAPTER 1

What is organic?

Why do I need to read this chapter?

A living investment

Growing your own fruit and vegetables in the backyard is rewarding but, even better, the fresh produce you harvest is good for you and your family. And if you can do it all without the use of chemicals, it is better for your health and the health of the environment. Here's how to get started and to keep on growing organically in your garden.

You want to grow fruit and vegetables in your own backyard and take an organic approach, which means no chemicals and nothing artificial. It sounds straightforward, but what does creating and maintaining an organic vegetable garden really mean?

The adjective 'organic' describes something that is, or once was, living. It is used to differentiate between material that is or was living (such

as you and me and the plants around us), and matter that is not or was not living (such as rocks and minerals). However, when it comes to gardening this definition doesn't really help us work out what is considered organic.

In terms of gardening, organic is used to mean growing plants without the use of manufactured fertilisers or harmful pesticides. It doesn't mean not applying any inorganic material, as inorganic materials include such things as rock minerals or even gravel mulches, which are quite acceptable in

organic gardening. In its broadest sense, however, the term 'organic' has an even bigger meaning for gardeners.

Organic is also used to refer to the way all living things are related to each other, and in a way this hints more at the meaning of the word when it is applied to gardening. Someone who is taking an organic approach to gardening is concerned with the inter-relationships between all the parts of their garden, from the soil to the plants to consuming the harvest.

The chain of life

To grow a plant organically means avoiding the use of artificial, chemical products in any stage of growth. Start as you mean to go on by preparing your garden with organic products, then planting organically raised seeds or seedlings, or larger plants that have been raised following organic principles.

As these organically derived plants grow it is important to control all the other inputs such as fertilisers and compost, as well as products used for disease and insect control, so that you are not applying unnatural and unnecessary chemicals to your garden.

Make sure you know the source of everything you add to your organic

LEFT Your organic garden not only supplies food for your table but helps to nourish itself by providing material to be composted and mulched and returned to the garden.

garden. To be a successful organic gardener you need to research all parts of the growing cycle.

As you start your organic garden, it will quickly become apparent that it is often difficult to source organic products. While an increasing number of organic products are sold through traditional nurseries and other retail outlets, many others must be bought at organic farmers' markets or from specialist organic suppliers.

Many organic suppliers have websites rather than shopfronts. To get you started we've listed details of current organic suppliers, including seed suppliers, in Chapter 13 (see page 191).

Site history

Before you even begin to make an organic garden, you need to get an idea of what's happened on the site previously, especially if the area was not gardened following organic principles. Chemicals of all sorts and from different sources can end up in soil to contaminate crops.

Such chemical residues can be present in soils if the site of your garden was once used for agriculture, commercial horticulture, industry or manufacturing. Even domestic activities such as home renovation can spill contaminants that can jeopardise organic growing, as can prior gardening activities. Your first move should be to check with the local council for previous land use. See box 'What was here before?' on page 14.

Organic labelling

As the term 'organic' can be defined in many ways, various groups involved in organic farming and production have implemented symbols to show they have met a particular group's organic standard. These standards will appear on organic products.

If you are unsure about the presence of chemicals in your soil, have it analysed to see what it contains. To do this, collect a soil sample (see 'How to take a soil sample' on page 12) and send it to a soil laboratory for analysis. To find a lab, check under 'Soil laboratories' in your local *Yellow Pages* or search for labs online. We also list some in Chapter 13 (see page 193).

If you are buying a property with the intention of growing plants following organic methods, have the soil sampled and tested as part of the pre-purchase investigations, just as you have termite and building inspections made.

Step-by-Step

HOW TO TAKE A SOIL SAMPLE

Your soil sample needs to reflect the type of soil in the area. Take a minimum of 5–10 samples per area. The depth to which you take samples depends on what you are planning to grow. They should be taken 10 cm deep for pasture and crops, and 15 cm deep for orchards and vineyards. For organic home gardens, take samples 10 cm deep.

1 Use a spade to dig a small hole with a vertical side.

2 Take a slice of soil about 2 cm thick to the required depth. Put it in a clean plastic bucket. Repeat this around the garden until you've taken the required number of samples.

3 Break up any clods and mix the samples together thoroughly.

4 Take a sample of around 200 g and send it to a soil laboratory for analysis.

General instructions

As well as getting the soil analysed for contaminants, have it checked for what it doesn't contain in the way of necessary nutrients and minerals (for details of the nutrients plants require, see 'Plant nutrients' on page 15). By knowing what's missing from the soil you can work to supply these minerals to help your plants to thrive.

Unless you have an understanding of soil chemistry, ask for the results to be interpreted for you in the form of a written report.

Basically, it is important to rule out the presence of heavy metals such as lead, cadmium or mercury that could be taken up by your plants as they grow and in turn be ingested by you and your family when you harvest and eat your crops.

If you discover there has been past contamination of your site, or even part of it, there are several things you can do to remedy the situation. You can have the contaminated soil removed and new, clean soil brought in to replace it. You can grow edible plants in the uncontaminated area. Alternatively, you can elect to garden in raised beds or containers, bringing in soil or organic garden mix. This approach leaves the contaminated soil on site but prevents exposure to the chemicals it contains.

RIGHT To avoid disturbing contaminated soils on your site, grow edible plants in raised garden beds using imported organic soil.

What was here before?

If you are planning to garden organically it is important to know the history of your site, to know what went on before you bought it. Here are some common prior activities that can contaminate soil.

Paint If the land was used for a commercial activity such as manufacturing paints or related products, spray-painting (for example, an automotive repairer) or if the house has had old paint removed and been repainted, the soil could be contaminated by heavy metals such as cadmium or lead.

Adjacent to a busy road Lead from exhaust emissions can accumulate in soil. Today's fuels are lead free but lead was used as an additive in petrol for many decades. Lead doesn't travel far from its source—such as the exhaust pipe of a car—so if your property is located on a busy road with lots of passing traffic avoid disturbing soil in the front garden. The soil behind a hedge, a solid fence or the house itself should be free of contamination.

Previous gardens Your proposed vegetable garden may have been someone else's lawn or rose garden, and therefore may contain residues from years of pesticide and fertiliser use.

Agriculture or horticulture Land on the outskirts of towns and cities may have been grazed or used for crops. Such soils could contain traces of pesticides such as organochlorides and herbicides.

Landfill sites The land may contain mixed materials that have been dumped as fill. It may contain toxins or wastes that are not compatible with organic growing.

What to do

- Have the soil tested for residues by a soil laboratory.
- Consider having contaminated soil removed.
- Build raised beds and grow your plants in certified organic garden mix from a reliable source.

RIGHT Before the introduction of unleaded petrol and ethanol, lead was emitted by vehicle exhausts and can still be found in soils adjacent to roadways.

Closed circle of nutrients

As well as providing healthy produce, gardening organically in your backyard reduces the amount of waste your household generates, which must be disposed of into landfill. Waste materials can be kept on site to be broken down and returned to the soil through a composting system, a worm farm or as mulch.

By re-using waste products such as kitchen scraps, garden prunings, lawn clippings and spent crops, you are reducing inputs to the garden so that less material is sourced from other sites. You also reduce the amount of garbage produced by your household. Instead of adding material to the garbage system, recycling nutrients by turning organic waste into garden mulch or compost keeps it out of the waste stream.

If you need to add to your soil things that you can't produce at home, try to source locally available products such as fertilisers, mulches or soil conditioners. Buying or sourcing locally cuts down on the need to use fuels to cart heavy or bulky materials over great distances.

Local sources of garden nutrients include stables (horse manure and straw for mulch), hobby farms (manure) or your council's green waste recycling system (compost and mulch). But always check the organic credentials of any outside product you source.

RIGHT Straw from spent crops or spoiled bales can be used as mulch to suppress weeds.

Plant nutrients

For growth, plants require the elements carbon (C), oxygen (O) and hydrogen (H), which are obtained from air and water. As well, twelve other elements, which are obtained from the soil, are also necessary. Some of the twelve are needed in large amounts (macro elements) while others are needed only in small amounts (micro or trace elements). Their availability to the plant may be limited by soil pH, by natural deficiencies in the soil, or by heavy uptake as the plant grows.

Other elements of benefit to plant growth are aluminium (Al), sodium (Na), cobalt (Co), vanadium (V) and silicon (Si). These are required in the very small amounts that are usually present in soil so do not need to be added.

ELEMENT (chemical symbol)	COMMENT
nitrogen (N)	major component of plant growth
phosphorus (P)	major component for most plants
potassium (K)	major component for most plants
calcium (Ca)	minor component
magnesium (Mg)	minor component
sulphur (S)	minor component
iron (Fe)	minor component
zinc (Zn)	trace element
copper (Cu)	trace element
manganese (Mn)	trace element
boron (B)	trace element
molybdenum (Mo)	trace element

Organic growing systems: permaculture and biodynamics

There are many methods of growing an organic garden. You can choose to cultivate a few vegetable beds following organic gardening methods, or turn your entire property over to an organic system of cultivation such as permaculture or biodynamics.

Many organic growers follow the permaculture system. The word was coined in Australia in the 1970s by Bill Mollison and David Holmgren by combining the words 'permanent' and 'agriculture' to describe a sustainable system of cultivation.

The idea of permaculture is modelled on the way plants, animals and their habitats naturally relate to each other and their surroundings. It is a system of growing that's ongoing and designed with the environment in mind. This organic system ties all living things to their environment to form one interrelated system that works with, not against, nature.

The permaculture system may be embraced on a balcony, a garden or a small farm. The concept (see 'Permaculture in a nutshell', right) has spread from Australia and is now followed by gardeners, horticulturists and farmers across the world in more than 120 countries.

To introduce permaculture to your garden or to better understand its principles, undertake a course, join a group or read more. There are books and websites about permaculture; for a list see Chapter 13, page 188.

Biodynamics, another approach to organic growing, was developed by Rudolf Steiner in Germany in the 1920s. It starts with the soil. Followers use specific additives called 'biodynamic preparations' to provide nutrients to crops by promoting biological activity in the soil. It is used in gardens, on smallholdings and farms. As well as adding special preparations, biodynamic gardeners and farmers follow traditional agricultural practices such as integration of livestock with crop and pasture rotation, tree planting, natural pest and disease control, the use of composted waste, and applying manure to their land. To find out more about biodynamics, and for details of relevant organisations and contacts, see Chapter 13, page 188.

LEFT Poultry play a fundamental role in all organic growing systems as they eat weeds and insects and provide fertiliser.

Permaculture in a nutshell

Permaculture takes a holistic approach to the layout, construction and planting of a garden. Twelve principles underlie a permaculture garden but here is a brief outline of the basic concepts relating to organic gardens.

Zoning Break the garden up into zones relating to the level of activity required (from most intensive to least intensive) and radiating out from a central point, such as the house.

Diversity Grow a large range of plants, mixing the crops together rather than using the traditional mass plantings of one species or variety. This helps to confuse pests and also attracts a wide range of the beneficial insects that aid pollination and pest control.

Animals Use animals as part of the garden. Poultry in particular has an important role to play in a permaculture system, from 'cultivating' areas prior to planting to foraging for pests and disposing of fallen fruit.

Maintenance Permaculture gardens are low maintenance, low cost and have low input from outside the ecosystem in which they operate. Mulching, composting and mixing up plantings help to reduce pests, weeds and the amount of hard work a garden usually demands.

Water The way in which water is used is fundamental to permaculture. Water is used and re-used, but it needs to be clean and free of pathogens. In a well-designed permaculture system water is collected, used, filtered through a biological system and re-used, often many times over.

CHAPTER 2

All about compost

Why do I need to read this chapter?

Composting basics

The compost heap is the engine room of an organic garden. It is the place to deal with organic waste and is a source of valuable nutrients. The key to successful composting is to get the heap working with the right amount of air and water, and at a high temperature for fast breakdown.

Making good compost is all about decomposition. This breakdown of organic materials occurs in two ways. It can be anaerobic or aerobic. Anaerobic decomposition stinks—both literally and for the environment. It takes place when material is broken down slowly by microorganisms called anaerobes, which function without the presence of oxygen. Ammonia, rotten egg gas (hydrogen sulphide) and methane are some of the unwelcome by-products of anaerobic decomposition.

Methane is one of the greenhouse gases that is contributing to climate change and global warming. Indeed, when it comes to global warming, methane is 21 times more destructive than carbon dioxide. If you are trying to do the right thing for the environment on your patch of Earth, anaerobic decomposition should be avoided.

Aerobic decomposition is the best way to make compost. Where there is plentiful oxygen during composting, such as in a home compost bin, aerobic decomposition occurs quickly and efficiently, turning organic waste into humus without producing methane. By-products of aerobic composting include water and some carbon dioxide, but the main product is rich, crumbly compost.

When compost is added to garden soil it continues to do good by absorbing carbon from the atmosphere and locking it away in your soil. This ongoing storage process is a form of carbon sequestration, which is at the heart of some carbon emission trading schemes.

The heat-loving or thermophilic microorganisms that are active in a warm, aerobic compost heap destroy disease-causing organisms. High temperatures also kill weed seeds, which makes your compost even more beneficial to your garden. The temperature at the centre of a well-functioning compost heap can reach 70°C, the temperature required to kill pathogens and weed seeds.

Making a compost heap

If you don't already have a compost heap, start one. You can make your own compost bin using bits and pieces of leftover materials (see 'How to build a compost heap', right) or buy a prefabricated bin or box.

Where you locate a compost heap is important for success. Select a spot that receives winter sun but has shade in summer. Under a deciduous tree is ideal.

If you've previously tried making compost and been less than successful, look at the new generation aerobic

ABOVE These bins have built-in aeration. Composted material is accessed from the base.

ABOVE Compost bins can be adapted from waste materials. This old bin easily holds prunings.

compost bins. Made of recycled plastic, they include vents and flues within the bin to encourage better aerobic decomposition.

The many different composting systems available at nurseries and hardware stores range from the basic black plastic cone to more upmarket models such as tumblers and aerobic systems. Used well, tumblers and aerobic systems speed up composting time.

Compost bins are open at the base and should sit directly on the soil. Don't stand a compost bin or try to make a compost heap on a hard surface such as paving or concrete. The bacteria, fungi and worms in the soil must have access to the heap as it is these organisms that turn unwanted organic matter into compost.

Once your productive organic garden is up and running, one

ABOVE Old pallets, set on their ends and lashed together, make a compost bin for garden waste.

compost bin will not be enough to cope with all your compostable material. Set up a system of three adjacent bins, so that you have one that's under way, one that's composting and one that's being used.

How to build a compost heap

Your compost heap can be a pile on the ground, or contained in a bin. If you are handy, make your own bin by recycling materials such as wooden pallets, iron sheeting or bricks.

You can adjust your homemade bin to suit your needs. The simplest method is to make a bay at least 1 m square and 1 m high. This size allows you to build up a volume of material that's large enough to heat up so composting can occur. Heaps smaller than this 1 m cubic size compost very slowly.

To make a simple bin, start by hammering four metal star pickets into the ground to form a square with sides of 1 m. Build up the back and side walls using bricks, timber or metal such as corrugated iron. Wire netting can also be used, but to prevent the heap from drying out the netting should be lined with cardboard or shadecloth. The front can be left open, or fitted with a removable wall for ease of access. For another method of composting, see 'How to make leaf mould in small spaces' on page 25.

What to put in your heap

Just about any organic material can be composted, from kitchen scraps, garden

prunings and leaves to cow, horse, goat and chicken manure. Also add old potting mixes, green weeds, pet hair and shredded paper. Some materials though should be kept out of compost heaps.

- Avoid adding scraps of food such as meat, dairy and bread, as they can attract vermin.
- Don't add pet droppings to your compost heap.
- Cardboard can attract termites. If your area is prone to this pest, don't use it to line your bin.
- Avoid large chunks of any type of material. Chop up food scraps and garden waste into small pieces, which break down much faster.

Faster working heaps

To speed up decomposition, chop as much material as possible into small pieces before adding it to the heap. Cut up prunings or put them through a mulcher, and use a spade to split citrus skins, which are often extremely slow to break down.

Spread large amounts of any one material over several layers by interspersing them with other

Tip   If you find something in your heap that's hasn't broken down, simply chop it up with the spade and return it to the heap to compost further.

materials. If you are adding a lot of something like grass clippings or wood ash, alternate them with kitchen scraps, leaves or green waste.

Most animal manures (horse, cow, sheep, goat, chicken, rabbit) can contain weed seeds. Either include such manures in a hot compost heap or use them as mulch that is regularly hoed to stop weeds from growing.

Know the source of all the organic matter you add. Don't compost weedy plants that are in seed or plants that can regrow from small pieces. Try to make 'hot' compost, so that any seeds are rendered sterile. Hot composts are those that reach 60–70°C.

Treat weeds in seed or those that grow from leaves, bulbs or rhizomes with caution and don't throw them into the compost without treatment. To stop the spread of weeds, steep in a bucket of water for a week or two, then add them to the heap. The water destroys the plant propagules, such as seeds or bulbs, so they can't germinate or regrow. For other methods of making compost heaps see 'How to make leaf mould in small spaces' on page 25.

To stop the spread of disease in your garden, avoid adding any diseased plant material (for example carrying diseases such as rust or mildew). This material should be binned or buried deep in the soil (at least 30 cm deep).

Unwanted visitors

While earthworms and the larvae of many beetle species, along with microorganisms and soil bacteria, are good to find in your compost heap, some other visitors are not welcome.

Rats are one unwelcome guest that may nest in a compost heap. You can keep them out by using a strong plastic compost bin with a lid, and making sure it sits firmly on the ground. Turn the heap regularly and avoid adding materials that are slow to break down.

Curl grubs are sometimes seen in compost heaps. These are the larvae of some beetles (see Chapter 11, page 167 for more details). While they are not a problem within a compost heap as they help the process of decomposition, they shouldn't be added to soils or mulches where plants are growing as they feed on plant roots. If you find any of these large, fat, C-shaped white grubs, feed them to your chooks.

Vinegar flies are also commonly found in compost heaps. They hover over the surface and can fly into your face when you open the lid. These are not fruit flies, pests that can destroy fruit, but benign creatures attracted by fermenting food scraps. If you find them offensive, deter them by sprinkling some soil or manure over the kitchen scraps, or just take their presence as an indication that it's time to turn the heap.

What to do with wood ash

A question that's often asked, especially in winter, is whether it's safe to put ash from slow combustion heaters on the garden or the vegie patch.

The answer is yes … *but*. Be careful where you put it and also make sure it is not HOT when you do spread it around, or you could find yourself responsible for the first bushfire of the season.

Wood ash is alkaline, so use it only around plants that tolerate lime. Lavender and roses will cope with wood ash. Never use it near plants that prefer acidic conditions—a group that includes most Australian native plants, along with azaleas, rhododendrons and acid-loving fruiting plants such as blueberries and citrus.

When you spread the ash, don't layer it too deeply (no more than 5 cm thick). Always water it in then lightly cover with a sprinkling of aged manure or compost. This stops it blowing around.

The alternative to spreading wood ash directly on the garden is to put it into the compost heap, adding a bucketful or so every couple of weeks along with your other compostable materials.

Step-by-Step

FIVE EASY STEPS TO GREAT COMPOST

As well as using the right materials in your compost, you have to balance the amount of air, water and nutrients. Composting is not an exact science, but the process works best if you follow a few basic rules. Here are some pointers to help you create top compost.

1 **Balancing carbon and nitrogen.** Some of the organic materials you add will be low in carbon but high in nitrogen; others will be high in carbon but low in nitrogen. An easy way to differentiate is to think of the compost ingredients as 'wet' or 'dry'. Wet materials such as food scraps, manures, green weeds and lawn clippings supply nitrogen. Dry materials such as shredded newspaper, mulches and dry leaves provide carbon. To give your compost the right balance, add about equal amounts by volume of each. For example, if you add a bucket of kitchen scraps (see picture 1, below), toss in a bucket of shredded paper as well. If you are adding large amounts of lawn clippings, intersperse them with woody prunings or dry leaves.

2 **Layering is good.** Making a compost heap out of alternating layers of 'wet' and 'dry' materials is a good way of getting the balance right. It's important to have a mix of ingredients. An easy way of getting it right is to always place a thin layer of manure (see picture 2, below) or kitchen scraps over a thicker layer of low-nutrient, bulky matter such as straw, leaves, bark, shredded paper or grass clippings. Don't feel you have to add all of everything at once. If you have a large amount of one type of material (say, grass clippings), add it to the heap gradually, interspersing it with other materials. If you have a lot of leaves, you can turn them into leaf mould instead of adding them all to the compost (see 'How to make leaf mould in small spaces', page 25).

3 **Keeping it damp.** Compost should be moist, like a damp sponge, but not wringing wet. If the heap appears too dry, add a sprinkle of water (see picture 3, below). If it is too wet, open it up to the air on warm dry days and cover it during long rainy spells.

4 **Aerating the heap regularly.** This is known as 'turning the heap' (see 'How to turn a compost heap' on page 24). It sounds complex, but is done simply by spading the material from one spot to another or by turning it using a tool called a compost worm (a spiral metal tool that looks like a giant corkscrew) or a fork.

5 **Giving it time.** The decomposition period varies with the time of year, the climate in which you live and with the make-up of any individual compost heap. With warm temperatures and good aeration (achieved by turning the heap frequently), compost can be ready to use in as little as three months. Generally, however, compost takes six months to a year to break down into a usable state (when it is often referred to as 'humus').

Compost calendar

With regular attention it is possible to have an active compost all year round. Here's your seasonal guide to tending your compost heap.

Spring The compost heap returns to life in spring as air and soil temperatures begin to warm. If you've neglected your heap over winter, get into action and turn it (see 'How to turn a compost heap', right).

Summer There are lots of materials to add to the compost heap throughout summer, particularly lawn clippings, prunings, green weeds and material from your vegie garden. The compost heap is best with summer shade. It may need to be wetted down from time to time in very dry weather, or covered with a lid or a tarpaulin in wet weather so it doesn't become saturated.

Autumn When adding lots of dry material such as leaves, add a sprinkle of manure and moisten the heap if necessary.

Winter When temperatures are low, compost heaps often fall by the wayside. There's a lot of good material around at this time of the year though, so don't let your heap languish. Continue to add fallen leaves, kitchen scraps, animal manure and a handful of lime. Cover the heap to allow it to warm up during the day.

How to turn a compost heap

One of the important techniques for managing compost is to keep it well aerated by regularly turning it. If you have a compost tumbler, all you have to do is turn a handle once or twice a day to aid decomposition. If you have your compost in a homemade frame or a bin, turn it with a spade or fork, or use a tool called a compost worm, thus stirring the material and allowing air to enter.

The easiest way to turn compost is to shovel or fork the contents of the heap into a new pile adjacent to the old one. If you have a compost bin, lift the bin up and move it to one side, then shovel all the material you've revealed back into it. If you have a compost bay, just turn the material within the bay.

As you work, use the shovel to chop up any large pieces, such as orange skins or bits of green woody growth, that are still intact. This helps them to break down.

With more oxygen available, aerobic activity multiplies, raising the temperature inside the compost heap and speeding up decomposition. To help the microbes along, add some animal manure. If your heap is on the nose, work in dolomite (lime).

Leaf mould

Fallen leaves and other organic materials that flow into our drainage systems are one of the biggest challenges to urban water management. This material flows straight into local creeks and waterways and, even though it's organic and 'natural', the decay process quickly depletes the oxygen in storm water and can lead to toxic algal blooms.

Rather than letting them go to waste, fallen leaves can be quickly, easily and cheaply turned into a form of compost or humus called leaf mould. If you only have a few leaves, add them into your normal compost bin, but if you have a surfeit such as occurs in autumn and winter in gardens with deciduous trees, make leaf mould.

Compost made entirely from fallen leaves is a rich source of nutrients. It can be dug into garden beds or applied as mulch. Gather a variety of leaves if you can, as each gives a different range of nutrients, and pile them into large bags (see 'How to make leaf mould in small spaces', opposite).

At other times of the year, you can gather fallen evergreen leaves such as gum leaves or pine needles. Evergreen materials such as these, however, break down very slowly.

For larger gardens, make a wire enclosure up to 1.5 m tall (which can be used for making any type of compost, not just leaf mould). Hammer four hardwood stakes or star pickets firmly into the ground to form a square with each stake about a metre apart. Secure the end of a roll of chicken wire to one of the posts with cable ties, which are easy to use. Unroll the netting around the posts as tautly as you can manage, fixing the cable ties as you go to secure the wire to each of the four corner posts. Cut away the excess netting with wire cutters and tuck away the sharp ends. To prevent spillage and retain moisture in the pile you can line the sides with cardboard, newspaper or old carpet. Fill the 'cage' with leaves, wet them down and soak the pile whenever it's dry. Push or trample the leaves down firmly when adding more.

Using compost and leaf mould

Don't just leave compost in the compost heap or leaf mould in bags. Use this nutrient-rich humus in your garden. It can be applied to the soil surface as mulch or dug into garden beds prior to planting.

If you need to add some compost to a garden bed but you feel your heap isn't completely ready, simply mine some of the brown and crumbly material from the bottom of the pile and use it in your garden.

Step-by-Step

HOW TO MAKE LEAF MOULD IN SMALL SPACES

In a small garden, the best way to make leaf mould is in large garbage bags. The warmer your climate, the faster the leaf mould develops—it can take from three months to three years depending on temperature. It's ready to dig into the soil when it's black and crumbly.

1 Rake up autumn leaves, gathering different species if you can.

2 Fill large garbage bags with the leaves, squirt in some water and tie up the tops.

3 Poke a few holes in the sides.

4 Tuck the bags away in a corner of the garden.

CHAPTER 3

Vegie garden basics

Why do I need to read this chapter?

Let's make a vegetable garden

The ideal site for a vegetable garden is an area that's in full sun, is level and has easy access, available water and shelter from cold, hot and dry winds.

OK, that's the ideal, but our real-life backyards are often very different from the ideal situation. They can be cramped, sloping and even shaded. In other words, they aren't always great for vegetable growing.

Don't despair—many of the vital conditions required for good vegetable growing (such as a level site, access to water and shelter) can be created and developed as the garden is established.

Sun, sun, sun

There is, however, one fundamental that must be met for success and that's access to sun. All productive plants grow best with lots of sunlight. To get maximum sunlight to your garden select a site that is open and not shaded by trees, buildings or other structures.

The more sunlight your garden receives the greater the range of plants that can be grown. Plants growing in sunny sites are also less worried by diseases—which in turn makes organic gardening a lot more successful.

In the southern hemisphere the sunniest sites are open to the north. North-easterly sites also get plenty of sun. In the northern hemisphere, the sunniest gardens face south, while south-easterly sites also get plenty of sunlight from early morning.

The exception to the rule of maximum sunlight is for plants growing in extremely hot summer climates. Here some shade is needed to protect them from dehydration. To allow year-round growth, however, the selected site should still be open and sunny, with shade provided during the hottest parts of the year by a shade system such as a shadehouse.

The amount of sunlight that falls over your garden varies depending on the time of the year. If you observe the path of the sun through the year you will notice it appears lower in the sky in winter than in summer, and rises in a different part of the sky in summer and winter. In fact, the sun is 47 degrees lower in the sky in mid winter than in mid summer, and sets in the west in a

Finding the sun

Use a compass to find north. You can easily buy a compass or, if you have a smart phone, check out its menu as many include a built-in compass. If you don't have a compass, check where the sun rises in the morning to find east. Then, if you stand so the sunrise (or eastern point) is to your right, you are facing north. The sun sets in the west, to your left. South lies behind you.

RIGHT To protect seedlings from the hot sun, erect a temporary cover such as this fleece-covered playpen.

different position in summer from that in winter. Areas of the garden that are cold and shaded in winter can be sunny in mid summer (and vice versa).

The term 'aspect' is used to describe a garden's orientation to the sun. If your backyard lies on the northern side of your house this part of the garden has a northerly aspect. Your front garden, being on the opposite side of the building, would have a southerly aspect.

ABOVE This permaculture-style garden is away from overhanging trees or buildings and has an open, sunny aspect for most of the day.

A level site

Vegetable gardens are easiest to maintain when they are created on a level site. If your garden is on a slope, create a level site for the vegetable bed with terraces. This is done by building retaining walls across the sloping site and back-filling them with extra soil to form a level bed.

The extra soil needed to fill the terraced bed can be brought onto the site by a landscape supplier, or taken from another part of your block that needs to be levelled. The method of using site soil to create an adjacent level space is known as 'cut and fill'. Many houses on sloping blocks are built on to a level space created through cut and fill.

For safety, retaining walls supporting a terraced bed should be less than 50 cm high. Walls higher than this must be planned and their construction supervised by an engineer to ensure they are safe. This is because they are holding back a large amount of soil. If the wall is not soundly built, it could collapse. Techniques to strengthen walls include battering—leaning the wall into the slope—and adding piers. Regulations vary, so check with your local council.

Retaining walls must be built with drainage holes at intervals along their base. These are known as 'weep holes' and ensure that water from rain or watering can drain away quickly. If water can't drain freely the wall may collapse under the combined weight of soil and retained water.

LEFT As the ground is sloping, this vegetable garden has been created in a raised bed so it is level with the lawn area behind.

RIGHT On this naturally level site the garden beds have been slightly elevated and contained by hardwood planks.

Tip When creating terraced beds allow plenty of level space adjacent to each bed to provide easy access to walk along and use safely. Allow at least 1–2 m so a wheelbarrow will fit along the path making it easier to carry materials.

To have access to the back of the bed, make terraced beds around 1.2–1.5 m wide. This isn't a magic number but the width you can reach by leaning across and extending your arm. Beds that are wider need to be accessed by standing in the bed or by reaching it from the other side, not always easy on a terrace.

As well as transforming a hard-to-work slope into a productive series of garden beds, terracing has the added benefit of allowing you to create raised garden beds which are easily accessible for working.

Garden plan

Before beginning to construct beds undertake soil preparation. This may be the only opportunity you'll get to use mechanical assistance. You can use machines such as rotary hoes to dig over the soil and to incorporate additional organic matter such as homemade compost or aged manure into the garden before planting.

To undertake major earthworks hire small diggers or a bobcat and operator to set out the garden.

If the area you are transforming into a vegetable garden is covered in turf or grassy weeds, flip to Chapter 9 (see page 132) for hints on how to remove weeds and grass following organic methods. Once the lawn is gone, dig over the soil, then rake it level to remove any remaining roots, grass runners or stones.

Designing your garden

Now you've located or made a sunny, level site on your block it's time to set out your basic vegetable garden.

A tape measure, pencil and paper, and graph paper and a scale ruler don't sound like gardening implements— but they will help you plan your garden. Draw up a plan if you need to calculate the amount of materials required to build your garden. Have a permanent plan to keep a record of plantings, or to design a formal potager-style garden with circular or wedge-shaped beds such as the one shown on page 36.

If you don't think you need to plan your vegetable garden on paper, do it in place, using anything to hand to set out the beds and path system in the shape and size needed. Useful materials can include your garden hose, timber bought for edging, stakes and stringlines, and a can of marking paint.

Fiddle around with the outlines of the beds until you are happy with the layout, and then begin to create the garden.

If you do decide to work out a plan on paper, measure up the area using the tape measure and note down the figures. Also note any relevant details such as the position of any fences, location of taps, existing paths and permanent plants such as trees.

With all the details on your rough sketch you can retreat indoors to transfer it to a scale plan on graph paper, working out how many beds you can fit in and making sure you leave space for paths.

Leave space between the garden beds for easy access. This should be at least 1 m wide, to allow the use of a wheelbarrow.

With a scale plan you can also work out how much material you need for fencing, surfacing the paths, edging the beds and any additional soil or organic matter required for filling them in.

Typically plans are drawn to a scale of 1:100 (that is, 1 cm equals 1 m on the ground) or 1:200 (1 cm represents 2 m on the ground) but you can select any scale you like. A useful trick is to cut out scale models of your proposed beds to see how they fit into the desired space before you head outside to start building them.

With your plan complete, mark out the area of the vegetable garden on the ground using a measuring tape and marking paint. This enables you to see whether the size you are planning actually works. Check that existing trees, uneven levels, paths and building shadows do not interfere with your layout, and adjust it if necessary.

Making a plan

You need these materials to draw up a garden plan.

- A tape measure
- Pencil and paper
- Graph paper and a scale ruler

RIGHT Make paths between beds wide enough to comfortably wheel a wheelbarrow.

Working to size

A vegetable garden can be as big or as small as you like, but there are a few basic principles that can help you work out the ideal size and to decide how many individual beds you want.

In commercial agriculture and also in horticulture, growing areas are designed for planting, maintaining and sometimes harvesting with the use of mechanical equipment. In these situations, vegetable growing areas may be several hectares in size and are often divided into fields.

In a home garden situation, where smaller amounts of many different crops are being grown and maintained by hand, garden beds are used to separate growing areas. In most cases four or six rectangular beds are sufficient. These fit into the average suburban backyard and allow for different crops to be grown in different beds in successive seasons. Moving the location of crops from season to season is called crop rotation and is discussed in more detail in Chapter 6 (see page 84).

The size and number of each garden bed created in the vegie patch is determined by several factors. The first is the total space available. The second is the amount of produce you want to grow. Producing enough vegetables to feed your family throughout the year will require more beds than just growing certain vegetables to supplement those bought from the markets or supermarket. Finally, keep your available time in mind.

BELOW In smaller garden beds grow small amounts of a range of different vegetables. Fast-growing vegies make the most of small spaces.

Step-by-Step

HOW TO MAKE A RAISED VEGIE BED

The best place to build a raised bed is somewhere flat and in full sun. If it's slightly sloping, dig away the high side until you have a level site, then clear away any rocks or debris. We used timber sleepers 2400 x 200 x 50 mm—four for each long side—to give us a finished height of 200 mm. Four more sleepers were cut in half (by the hardware store) for the short ends.

1 Place the first layer on the ground. Start with one long piece and an end piece butted up to it. Check the level. Add or remove soil from under the sleepers until they are completely level.

2 Lay the sleepers for the other two sides and check the level again. Adjust the soil level if needed.

3 For the next layer, place a short end piece first. Position it so that it overlaps the end of one of the long side sleepers, rather like laying bricks. Position the other three sides, making sure they are square to the bottom layer.

4 Drill three holes in one corner of the sleepers—one right in the corner and one either side. It's best to do one corner at a time, as the sleepers can move while you're hammering and the holes will shift out of alignment.

5 Hammer decking nails into each drill hole. Repeat for the other three corners.

6 Continue building, making sure you overlap the sleepers at the corners. Secure with the decking nails every layer until you've reached your desired height. Fill with soil.

Vegie gardens and trees

If your garden includes some large established trees, read on. Trees and vegetable growing don't mix. This is due in part to the shade the trees cast, but also their ability to compete with vegetables for food. Most trees possess an extensive root system which is always searching for food and water. A vegetable bed built on or near a tree's root system will usually produce inferior crops due to competition from the roots. Such beds will also need more water to grow.

If you have no option but to garden under or near trees, follow these tips.

1 Select the sunniest area to establish your garden—usually on the north side of the tree in the southern hemisphere or the south side in the northern hemisphere.

2 Use a raised bed. The more robust the trees, the higher the raised bed needs to be. Place a barrier between the soil for your vegetables and the tree roots. This could be a commercial root barrier dug into the soil or geotextile fabric, natural fibre carpet or matting laid at the bottom of the raised garden bed. If old carpet or matting is used be sure to check it is compatible with organic principles.

3 Cover the crop with a net to catch falling leaves, twigs and branches.

The size of each vegetable bed is also determined by the type of edging material used. If you are planning to have a spaded edge, scale is not critical, but if you are making a raised bed or edged bed, relate the total length of the bed to the module size you are using. For example if your timber is 2 m long, make your bed 2 x 1 m (see page 38 for common modular lengths). This reduces complexity and allows beds to be constructed quickly and efficiently.

Vegetable beds can be built with brick, stone or, for a fast option, straw bales. Alternatively, buy beds prefabricated in corrugated iron, or pre-cut beds made from timber or polymer. These usually come in set

RIGHT To mark out a circular bed (such as shown here), place a stake in the centre of the bed and attach a length of string equal to the bed's radius. Attach a short stake to the string and inscribe the circle in the ground as you walk.

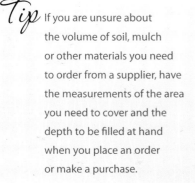

Tip If you are unsure about the volume of soil, mulch or other materials you need to order from a supplier, have the measurements of the area you need to cover and the depth to be filled at hand when you place an order or make a purchase.

sizes but other types are modular so several can be joined together to create a larger garden area. For an idea of how to make a raised vegetable garden, see our step-by-step construction guide on page 35.

To avoid over-ordering or under-ordering materials, draw up a plan before you start (see page 32) or measure the beds carefully. For edging, work out the perimeter of each bed, which is (length + width) x 2. If you are making a raised bed, work out the height you want the bed to be (for example, 200 mm or 300 mm) and decide how many rows of timber or courses of bricks will be needed to reach that height.

RIGHT This small, level garden bed is edged with bricks set into the soil. These divide planting areas, provide access and are decorative.

Why grow in beds?

All this concern about creating vegetable beds may seem like a lot of hard work. Surely you can simply plant vegetables and let them grow wherever they are happiest?

This informal approach works well if you are growing only a few vegetables in a larger garden, if your entire garden is informal, or you are following a permaculture system which mixes up plantings.

Other than these exceptions, it is much easier to plant, maintain and harvest vegetables grown in distinct beds that are regular in size and shape.

Modular sizes

This table gives you a general idea of the sizes of basic building materials to aid in planning the size of garden beds. Sizes may vary, so check with your local building supplier or recycling yard.

Material	Size in mm (L x W x H)	Comment
brick	230 x 110 x 76 (Australian standard)	brick dimensions vary with place of manufacture but usually a brick's length is twice its width (including a mortar joint of 10 mm)
Besser block	390 x 90 x 190	also available at 140 mm, 190 mm widths
treated pine sleeper	2400 x 200 x 50	other sizes available; sleepers can be cut to any length
straw bale	900 x 450 x 350	these bales are called 'two-string bales'
corrugated iron	820 x 0.42 (width x thickness)	cut to length, width of sheets is measured in terms of coverage, so a standard 820 mm sheet is sold as 762 mm wide with 58 mm coverage; gauge or thickness varies: roofing sheets are 0.42 mm, fencing sheets 0.35 mm

BELOW Raised beds allow you to create a vegetable bed anywhere there's enough level space. They are also easy to work at without bending. In hot areas shade the sides with companion plants or shade cloth.

As with the size of the bed, relate the bed height to the size of the unit you are using. For example, a brick is 76 mm high so a garden bed made with three courses of bricks, including 10 mm mortar, will be around 258 mm high. If you are using recycled timber, railway sleepers or treated pine logs, measure their height and use this as the basis for estimating the height of the bed.

To order extra organic garden mix or soil to fill the beds, or mulch to surface them, work out the volume you need to obtain by calculating length x width x height (see above, 'Modular sizes').

This is best done in metres, giving you an answer in cubic metres.

If you have to pay for delivery and the volume of soil you need is less than one cubic metre it may be easier and cheaper to buy organic garden mix in bags. It's also better to buy bags if access to the garden is difficult and the material has to be carried to the site, or if you have nowhere to store it, as it is easier to manage and unlikely to be invaded by weeds. However, if the bags are left too long in the sun the plastic breaks down due to the effects of UV light and becomes brittle.

Tip If you have a large amount of organic garden mix, soil or mulch delivered and can't use it immediately, cover it with a tarpaulin to prevent it from being contaminated by any weed seeds that are blown in from surrounding areas.

Existing garden

If you have an area that's already been used as a vegetable garden you may simply need to do a bit of renovation—repairing edgings, reinstating pathways and fences, and weeding. Previously used vegetable gardens will benefit from the addition of organic material to reinvigorate the soil.

In some instances vegetable gardens are abandoned because they become unsuited to their purpose. Before you spend time renovating, check that an abandoned vegetable garden isn't overshadowed by trees or surrounding buildings, poorly drained or difficult to

BELOW Established beds may just need tidying and extra organic matter dug in, but if they are overshadowed relocate them to a sunnier spot.

access. If it is shaded, particularly in the morning, it is sensible to select a new area to build your vegie patch.

No-dig gardens

No-dig gardens are quick and easy to construct (see the step-by-step guide on page 40) and are a simple alternative for gardeners with soils that are not suitable for growing vegies. They are also ideal for people with limited mobility as they don't involve heavy digging and are raised to an easily accessible height. Most vegies and herbs can be grown in a no-dig garden.

No-dig gardens can be built on top of most surfaces, such as lawn, an existing garden bed or even paving or concrete. The no-dig concept is also a great way to fill a raised bed. The no-dig garden is made from alternating

layers of dry high-carbon materials, such as shredded prunings, dry leaves and straw, and high-nitrogen materials, such as fresh grass, manures and lucerne. Each layer should be around 10 cm thick. Apply a generous amount of blood and bone after each dry layer to help speed up decomposition. Water in each layer as you go. At this stage the garden should be 60–80 cm high.

In a week or two, as it begins to decompose, the garden will settle to around half its original height. Wait for this settling to occur before planting crops. Over time, top up with new layers of lucerne, manure and compost, so the height stays at about 30–40 cm.

However, if you want to plant seeds or seedlings immediately, create little planting pockets in the bed and fill them with organic potting mix., then plant into the pockets.

Step-by-Step

HOW TO MAKE A NO-DIG GARDEN

1 Mark out the area for the no-dig garden. If you are building it on top of lawn or weeds, kill the existing vegetation by applying a generous amount of blood and bone and garden lime, and watering them in well. Alternatively, remove the grass using a spade or turf cutter.

2 Spread out sheets of newspaper to deprive the weeds or lawn of light. Lay at least ten sheets thick and overlap. Water.

3 Start by adding a layer of the coarsest material, such as dry leaves and woodchips. Sprinkle over with blood and bone. Water gently.

4 Add a layer of high-nitrogen material, such as manure.

5 Continue adding alternating layers until you reach the required height. When you near the top, alternate with a couple of layers of lucerne and manure.

6 Finish off with a layer of compost, then water in well. Wait for a couple of weeks before planting.

Fences and barriers

Fences provide protection from pests (such as rabbits, deer, kangaroos, wallabies), pets, particularly dogs, or livestock including chickens, sheep, goats and cattle.

You can make your own fences using recycled materials such as wire, timber or even pallets, or you can employ a fencing contractor. Professional fencing is not cheap. Prices start at around $25 per metre.

The size and strength of the fence you construct must relate to what you are trying to contain (or exclude). If you are trying to keep out livestock, the fence needs to be around 1.2 m high. Sturdy fence posts and four or five strands of strong wire are required to exclude large animals. You may also need mesh fencing to exclude smaller animals such as the neighbour's dogs and your own pets.

If you are only excluding rabbits, the fences don't need to be as high or as substantial. Run lengths of chicken-wire netting about 50–60 cm high around your vegetable garden, securing it to stakes. Make sure it is also secure at its base to stop rabbits getting underneath. Use wire hooks to fix the netting to the ground.

Where kangaroos and birds are a problem, consider enclosing each vegetable bed with a meshed-in cage.

Whatever type of fence you select, remember to include an easily opened gate for access to and from your crops.

BELOW Netting has been loosely draped around and secured to protect the vegies from wallabies.

BOTTOM, LEFT A permanent, sturdy fence and gate excludes large animals from this vegie plot.

BOTTOM, RIGHT This low band of mesh is being used to deter rabbits from feeding on the vegies.

Paths

The type of path surfacing you use in a vegetable garden can be critical to the garden's success. The path needs to be trafficable in all weathers but particularly during and after rain. Even daily watering of the vegetable garden can cause paths to become wet and difficult to access if they are poorly constructed or built of unsuitable material.

LEFT Bricks and pavers make long-lasting and durable paths that are accessible in all weathers. Lay so water drains into the beds during rain.

As well as walking on paths you may need to use them when moving wheelbarrows or even heavy equipment, so take future use into account when the path is being built. Create a solid base for a path that will take a lot of traffic or that needs to resist heavy wear.

Paths that can be walked on even in wet weather are usually, but not always, made from solid materials such as concrete, bitumen or paving.

Wooden planks can make useful paths over wet or soggy soils, as can a thick layer of sawdust, crushed concrete, pebbles, gravel, ash or granite.

Where a granular material such as granite or coarse sand is used, it should be laid on a firm base and, if possible, mechanically compacted to make it firmer to walk on, longer lasting and more durable in wet weather. This also helps prevent weed growth.

Raised paths stay drier than paths level with the ground and also allow water to drain into the surrounding beds, but they are expensive and difficult to build. Sunken paths may stay wet for prolonged periods after rain or watering and so need to be surfaced with firm materials such as bricks or pavers.

ABOVE For all-weather gravel paths, compact the soil well before laying the gravel or incorporate cement in the gravel mix and then compact.

ABOVE Recycled mulch makes a soft and inexpensive path but use edging to keep the material on the path and out of the surrounding beds.

CHAPTER 4

Orchards and fruit production

Why do I need to read this chapter?

The fruit garden

A collection of fruit-bearing trees is known as an orchard. Orchards can be planted with fruit or nut trees and bushes, and may be composed of one type of fruit or, more usually in a home garden or hobby farm, of a mixture of different types of fruits.

Orchards can be given various names depending on their size and the types of fruiting plants they contain. A large orchard of nut trees, tropical fruit trees or coffee is called a plantation, while tea is grown in a tea garden. Orchards of citrus or olives are usually referred to as groves. A planting of nut-bearing trees such as hazelnuts may be referred to by the delightful term 'nuttery'.

Whatever its name, an orchard is a way of growing fruit trees so they are easy to manage and ensuring that trees are in close enough proximity to each other for the purpose of cross-pollination (see page 53 for more information about pollination and flowering in productive plants).

For ease of maintenance and harvesting, fruit-bearing trees are usually grown in rows with even spacing between each tree and then regular spacing between each row. The overall effect is of a grid of trees.

Orchards are fenced or hedged to keep out animals that may damage the trees or feed on the crops.

In commercial horticulture, orchards can be vast, covering many hectares. Almond orchards in California, for example, stretch for kilometres. But smaller orchards are also commercially viable—for example, the Sorrento lemons traditionally grown in southern Italy for limoncello are squeezed into small spaces on terraced hillsides.

That's the practical picture of an orchard, but for most home gardeners an orchard is a much more romantic notion. It is easy to envisage the joy of wandering among productive trees, plucking fruit or enjoying the trees in flower and buzzing with bees.

Orchards flourish in art and literature, and gardens throughout history. These images are likely to shape our idea of how our own orchard may look. But, for good fruit production, keep practicalities in mind as you plan your orchard.

LEFT An orchard of apples and crabapples has been set along a path and underplanted turning a productive garden into a place of beauty.

RIGHT Orange and other citrus don't need cross-pollination so can be grown as stand-alone trees in an ornamental garden.

How much space?

In an average garden you probably won't have room for a dedicated orchard. But by choosing dwarf varieties, or through regular pruning and training, productive fruit trees can be grown in small spaces beside a driveway, on a nature strip, along a fence or even in pots. Fruit trees can be used to hedge a productive garden. For more on productive planting in small spaces, see Chapter 5.

The mini-orchard is becoming increasingly popular with gardeners in urban areas as the range of dwarf fruit trees increases. These may be small cultivars, or trees grafted on to a dwarfing or low-growing rootstock (for more on grafting and rootstocks, see 'What is grafting?', left).

However, to grow enough fruit to feed your family throughout the year, larger trees are needed. When assessing how much space your desired collection would require, consider their mature size, particularly their spread. This information may be included on plant labels—but be warned, it is often underestimated. Labels may list plant size after five years' growth, rather than at maturity after seven to ten years' growth.

The ultimate size of a tree is determined by its rootstock, and by soil type along with growing conditions, particularly the availability of nutrients and water. Trees grown in poor soil with periods of drought or insufficient water are usually smaller than their better provided for counterparts in other areas. Trees that are closely planted may also be smaller.

To work out the minimum spacing between fruit trees, allow for growth in each direction and plant them at half their canopy width apart from the spread of the next one. (For example, if tree A will spread to 3 metres, and tree B to 2 metres, allow half of 3 metres plus half of 2 metres between them—that is, 1.5 + 1 m = 2.5 m.) If space is at a premium, plant more closely and with regular pruning prevent the trees from growing to their full size.

What is grafting?

Plants have a root system, stem/s and leafy growth. When plants grow from a seed or a cutting, this growth is all one plant. However, many plants can be grafted together so that the root system of one supports wood taken from another plant or even several others. When this is done, the plant that supplied the root system is called the rootstock. The upper part of the plant is called the scion or graft.

Grafting in human medicine, for example skin grafts, is done to repair damage or totally replace a defective part of the body. Grafting in horticulture is done to produce a stronger plant, to reproduce a desirable variety, or to control plant size. Often it achieves all three. Plants that have been damaged can also be repaired or rejuvenated with grafting. Both ornamental and productive plants are grafted.

Growers select a plant with a strong root system for the understock. These plants are often grown from seed but can also be propagated from cuttings. Once the plant is growing strongly—around two years—a piece of stem from another plant is attached to the upper growth of the understock. This may be done by removing all the plant's own growth and inserting wood from another plant in its place, or by adding smaller pieces of a new plant to the top growth. This type of grafting is often termed 'budding'.

Grafting can be done low down on the plant or higher up. Usually there is a difference in colour and sometimes diameter between rootstock and scion so you can tell when and where a plant is grafted. To grow a grafted plant it is important to maintain the top growth and remove any shoots that may appear from the understock, below the graft.

The point on the stem at which the scion meets the understock is called the graft union.

Organic orchard

For organic gardeners, an orchard is more than a convenient place to grow fruiting trees, it is an integral part of an organic growing system.

Ideally orchards are integrated with animal production. Sheep and pigs can be good companions for orchards. They help to clear up fallen fruit, which often contains pests, in addition to acting as natural lawnmowers by cropping grass and weeds beneath trees and between rows. Animals also add their manure to the ground, helping to feed and nurture the trees.

Poultry are also excellent natural companions for orchards. Geese, ducks and chickens that are allowed to forage among the trees keep grasses and weeds down, and eat fallen fruit and insects. Guinea fowl are particularly good at reducing insect populations, especially hard-to-catch insects such as grasshoppers.

However, animals such as goats, horses and cattle can be detrimental to the wellbeing of an orchard as they can strip bark, break branches or even feed on unharvested fruit. Large animals may also compact the soil around trees, which may cause damage to roots.

Beehives, on the other hand, are natural orchard companions. The bees visit flowers, carrying pollen from one plant to the next and so ensure that crops form. In exchange, the bees collect nectar and pollen, which is taken back to the hive for honey production. The European honeybee (*Apis mellifera*) is the bee most commonly found in orchards. Bumblebees (restricted in Australia to the island state of Tasmania) and native bees can also carry out pollination.

BELOW Poultry are useful in orchards for clearing up fallen fruit and pest insects.

Fruit all year round

While many commercial orchards contain just one type of fruit tree (such as apple, avocado or pecan), a home orchard is usually planted with a mixture to provide a range of fruit.

With careful planning, it is possible to have an orchard that can provide some sort of fruit all year round. This is achieved by planting different types of trees, and including varieties which crop at different times in the season.

To achieve a harvest for every month of the year, plant trees that give fruit in different seasons and grow several varieties of each type to extend the harvest. Varieties are usually described as early, mid or late season to indicate in which part of the season they are ready to harvest. An early season peach, for example, may be ready to harvest in late spring while a late season peach may not ripen until mid summer.

To plan your orchard refer to the table 'Fruit all year', which lists popular fruit trees and peak production season.

As well as planting a range of trees for harvesting throughout the year, also consider how suitable the fruit you grow is for storage—either as fresh fruit or preserved by drying, bottling or freezing. Apples, for example, can be harvested over many months but also stored and eaten later.

LEFT Growing early, mid and late season apricot varieties extends harvest from spring to summer.

Fruit all year
POPULAR FRUITS FOR BACKYARDS

Note: Exact harvest times will vary, so use this table as a guide only. Select fruits that suit your climate zone.

FRUIT	SUMMER			AUTUMN			WINTER			SPRING		
	DEC	JAN	FEB	MAR	APR	MAY	JUNE	JULY	AUG	SEPT	OCT	NOV
Apple		■	■	■	■	■						
Apricot	■	■										■
Avocado	■				■	■	■	■	■	■	■	■
Banana	■	■										■
Blueberry	■	■										
Fig			■	■	■							
Grapefruit						■	■	■	■	■	■	■
Grapes		■	■	■	■	■						
Guava					■	■						
Lemon	■	■	■	■	■	■	■	■	■	■	■	■
Loquat	■								■	■	■	■
Mandarin						■	■	■	■			
Mulberry	■									■	■	■
Nectarine	■	■	■									
Orange	■						■	■	■	■	■	■
Passionfruit	■	■	■	■	■	■						
Peach	■	■										
Pear			■	■	■	■	■					
Persimmon				■	■	■						
Plum	■	■	■									■
Strawberry	■	■							■	■	■	■

Community orchard

Because many types of fruiting trees produce a larger harvest than one family can consume, there have been attempts in different parts of the world to plant community orchards so produce is freely available to all.

These may be established in public places as street trees, or in parks or semi-public places such as school and university grounds.

In Seville in Spain, the streets are planted with Seville oranges, a bitter orange with a short cropping time, which is used for making marmalade and preserves.

Community orchards can also be established in or around community vegetable gardens. In the United Kingdom, community apple orchards have been planted in some areas to provide both fruit for the surrounding inhabitants and to provide a space to grow rare or heritage varieties.

The downsides of community orchards, school and street plantings are difficulties that arise in the management of pests and diseases, and the problems caused when the fruit

isn't harvested regularly and is allowed to fall to the ground and rot.

Site selection

Most fruit trees have similar needs so they can be grown successfully in a mixed orchard. Fruiting plants grow best in rich, well-drained soil in a sunny position with protection from strong winds.

In areas with low annual rainfall, or with strongly seasonal rainfall such as occurs in both tropical and Mediterranean climates, fruit trees may require irrigation in dry times to crop well. Access to a reliable water supply is an important consideration when an orchard is being planned and its location decided.

Orchards also need to be accessible for maintenance and harvest. In a small orchard the work can be done by hand but in a larger area mechanical assistance is required, particularly for maintaining the areas between the trees.

LEFT The ornamental Bradford pear is often used as a street-planting tree. Its fruit can be used for making jams and sauces.

BELOW Pawpaws have male and female flowers on separate plants. Both are needed for fruit to form on the female plant.

Where mechanical equipment is to be used, ensure that the trees are spaced far enough apart to allow the use of a mower or small tractor.

Pollinators

For good crops to form, most fruit trees need another tree to provide pollen to fertilise its flowers in a process known as cross-pollination. Most fruit trees are insect pollinated and it is usually bees that carry pollen from one tree to another. Others, including many nut trees, are wind pollinated.

Some fruit trees carry the cross-pollination process one step further by having separate male and female flowers on the same plant. This type of flowering plant is referred to as monoecious. The male flowers have only pollen-bearing parts while the female flowers contain the ovary, which forms the fruit. Many pine trees, some species of fig and in the vegie garden, corn, are monoecious.

In other species, male and female flowers are produced on separate plants. These species are termed dioecious. Persimmons, bananas, pawpaws and kiwifruit, for example, are dioecious.

To produce fruit from dioecious plants it is necessary to have at least one male and one female plant. In most cases one male plant will be sufficient to pollinate four to eight female plants. In some cases male and female plants are grafted on the same rootstock; self-fertile varieties may also be available.

Chilling needs

As well as requiring cross-pollination for fruit production, some fruiting trees also require 'chilling' to ensure flowering and fruiting.

Fruit-bearing trees that are dormant during winter often need to experience a certain number of hours of chilling to bring on flowering. This need for chilling prevents them from flowering too early.

Citrus trees and tropical fruit trees do not have a chilling requirement, but other commonly grown fruits such as apples, pears, cherries, peaches and nectarines do need a cold winter.

Chilling refers to a specific number of hours below 7°C. These hours are accumulated during winter as the trees are exposed to cold nights. The hours of chilling needed varies with species and variety, and ranges from 300 to 1200 hours. Plants are described as having high, medium or low chilling needs. In warm climates choose fruit trees with low chilling needs (around 300 hours) or crop production will be poor or non-existent.

To find out the number of chilling hours common to your area, check with your local bureau of meteorology. Also note what types of fruit trees are grown successfully in your area—your local nursery, garden club or botanic garden should be able to provide this sort of regional information.

Planting fruit trees

As fruit trees are long-term plants, it is worth investing time in site preparation and planting. When planting, dig a hole that's as deep as the root ball and two to three times the width. This would generally mean creating a hole around 1 m across and 50 cm deep. If you are planting a bare-rooted tree, build up a mound of soil in the base of the hole on which to sit the roots. This is done to avoid creating air pockets around the root ball, which can stunt root growth.

Before planting incorporate well-rotted compost into the base of the hole, and mix some more compost

RIGHT Most apples have chilling needs but varieties sold as tropical apples fruit after only 300 chilling hours so suit warm winter areas.

LEFT After planting a grafted tree spread organic mulch around to keep the soil moist, root system cool and reduce weed competition. As the mulch breaks down it also helps to nourish the tree.

with the soil dug from the hole (this is used to firm the tree into the planting hole, a process called back-filling). You can also add minerals at this stage, including phosphorus (1 kg per tree of rock phosphate is recommended) and trace elements (around 100 g per tree).

Before planting a bare-rooted tree, check the root system and prune back any damaged roots. Avoid exposing the root system to the air for any length of time: this can lead to dehydration, which could cause the plant to establish slowly, fail to thrive or even lead to its death.

A good tip is to soak both bare-rooted and potted plants in water to which a seaweed tonic has been added before planting. This keeps the plant fully hydrated during the planting process.

The seaweed tonic absorbed from the water also helps reduce transplant shock. The water can then be used to water the tree in after planting.

Plant so the tree is sitting at the same depth in the soil as it was previously (whether in the ground or a pot), and water it in, firming the soil around the roots (see 'How to plant a grafted tree', right). If you are planting a grafted tree, the graft or bud union (clearly indicated on the trunk by a change in bark colour) should be at least 10 cm above ground level.

Step-by-Step

HOW TO PLANT A GRAFTED TREE

1 Dig a hole the same depth as the root ball and about twice as wide. Add compost to the base of the hole. If the tree is potted, remove the pot, and place the root ball in the hole.

2 Lay a stake across the top of the hole to check that the surrounding soil is at the same level as the top of the root ball. If you're planting a bare-rooted tree, there will be a change in colour on the trunk that indicates the previous soil level. Any graft should be about 10 cm above soil level.

3 Mix a bucketful of well-rotted homemade compost, or about half a bag of purchased organic compost, into the soil that's been dug out of the hole.

4 Back-fill the hole, making sure that the soil is pushed right down into the gap between the root ball and the surrounding soil. Water well.

How to stake a tree

Although dependence on a stake can weaken a tree in the long-term, stakes can give vital support in windy locations or where a large tree is being transplanted. In these cases use two, or better still three stakes for support. Place two stakes on either side of the tree or spread three equally around the tree and drive them into the soil. Place stakes out from the trunk and beyond the root ball. Use hessian webbing or budding tape to hold your tree in place, tying it securely to the stakes using a figure-8 pattern so that it can still flex in the wind and strengthen naturally. After your tree has grown into its new position, remove the stakes. As an alternative to a stake, erect shelterbelts in the form of temporary hessian barriers.

If the tree is exposed to winds, stake it at planting time to reduce damage that can be caused by wind rock. Three, or even two stakes provide the best support for the tree (see 'How to stake a tree', left).

The stakes also provide a structure around which you can wrap hessian webbing, plastic or chicken-wire netting to give the new plant protection from wind, frost or browsing animals.

Use soft ties such as tree ties (available from organic suppliers, nurseries and some hardware stores), raffia or recycled pantihose to tie the tree to the stakes. Whatever material you use, do not tie it tightly around the trunk to allow movement.

Check stakes and ties regularly, loosening ties as the tree grows to avoid damage to the trunk. Also at planting, remove any plant labels or ties added by the nursery.

Pruning needs

Bare-rooted trees are pruned at planting when they are dormant as the first step in shaping for fruiting and ease of ongoing care and harvest.

Although most types of fruit tree have specific pruning requirements, the general aim is to create an open vase-shaped tree that is small enough to allow all branches to be reached for harvesting and to make netting for bird-control manageable. Vase-shaped trees have three to five main branches and are open in the centre to allow good air circulation through the plant.

Where you are planting a multi-branching tree, cut each branch back to encourage growth and remove the main leader (main growing point) to open up the centre of the tree. Ongoing maintenance would involve removing inward-growing branches.

Fruit trees can also be pruned to have a central leader and several side branches. This shape is effective for a tree grown in a narrow space or as an espalier. To do this, cut the main leader back by about a third to encourage side branches. Cut to just above a node.

Between the lines

Once you have decided on the fruit trees for your orchard, and established their spacing and pollination needs, there are still several factors to consider.

Windfalls and discarded fruit

Fallen fruit or windfalls can harbour pests and diseases, so they should be removed either by allowing animals or poultry to browse among the trees or by raking it up and using it in compost or to feed stock. Windfalls of apples and pears can be used to make juice, or fermented to make alcoholic cider and perry.

Companion plants

What you do between the rows of fruit trees in an organic orchard is an important consideration, as your choice will affect both maintenance and crop management. Orchards can be mulched, grassed or planted with herbs and flowers. Often it is best to do all three. Maintain a cleared area under each tree, which can be spread with mulch to deter weed growth. Grow grass between the rows—it can be mown or cropped to allow easy access to the trees for maintenance and harvesting. Flowering plants such as herbs or wildflowers will attract both pollinators and beneficial bugs. These can be sown with the grass or planted throughout the orchard.

BELOW Prune fruit trees from planting to encourage an open, vase shape with a framework of three to five main branches.

Mistletoe

Sections of growth that are different from the rest of a fruit tree are probably mistletoe. Mistletoe is a plant parasite that can be found on fruit trees such as apples as well as on many native Australian species, including gum trees. There are around 70 species of mistletoe in Australia. A healthy tree can normally cope with mistletoe infestation, but an old or weakened tree may suffer or even die.

If you don't want the mistletoe it can be pruned out. Mistletoe seeds are spread by mistletoe birds, and controlled by small mammals such as sugar gliders, which arrive to feed on the flowers and leaves at certain times of the year. A healthy population of native birds and animals can reduce infestations. Mistletoe is also used by small birds as a nesting site.

Crop protection

One of the most difficult parts of growing your own fruit is keeping it on the tree long enough to ripen. Birds, bats and insects are all poised ready to eat your crop before it is ready to harvest.

The only successful and organically friendly way to keep large pests away is to net or cage your fruit trees, shrubs and vines. Soft berry fruits in particular are so readily damaged that it is difficult to produce a crop in many areas without a fruit cage.

While netting a fruit tree as the crop matures may seem a straightforward way of deterring birds, it can have a host of problems. As well as it being difficult and costly to net large trees, birds, bats and reptiles can become tangled in the net. To make netting easier for you and safer for wildlife, follow these pointers.

- Keep trees pruned to an easy height and width so netting is possible.
- Erect a simple structure around each tree so the net can be stretched over it and above the tree. This approach reduces damage to wildlife. Use bent PVC tubes secured on star pickets or build a wooden frame.
- Use woven shadecloth or 40 mm white knitted netting (stretched taut). Avoid open black or dark polyethylene netting (called monofilament). This black netting is hard for animals to see and causes many injuries.
- Net lower branches of big trees or throw shadecloth over the part of the tree you can reach and peg it into position on the branches.
- Draw netting tightly over the tree to make it less likely that animals can become trapped or tangled in it.
- Avoid leaving large amounts of loose netting on the ground. Netting that reaches the ground should be stretched taut and pegged in place.
- Each day check all parts of the net, including its base. Check the net more frequently in hot weather or if animals are about. If a trapped

LEFT Figs and berry fruits are a magnet to birds. Protect them under a chicken wire frame.

animal has been injured, call your local wildlife rescue service (see Chapter 13, page 193 for contacts) or take it to a vet for assessment and treatment.

The use of netting and fencing is also a useful way to keep animals such as kangaroos and wallabies, as well as introduced deer and rabbits, out of orchards. Wire fences around an orchard or fruit-growing area or low barriers made from chicken wire or shadecloth can keep these animals away from fruit trees. You can also protect individual young trees from browsing animals by enclosing them with some type of barrier.

Vines and berries

Vine fruits such as grapes and passionfruit, and berry plants such as raspberries, blueberries and any of the bramble berries (including blackberries), are planted and managed in much the same way as fruiting trees.

Vines, particularly grapevines, require a structure on which to climb. Vines can be planted to hedge or fence a garden, vegetable patch or to surround an orchard.

Strawberries are the smallest of all the berry plants. They are an ideal choice for growing in a backyard and can be fitted into even a small garden. They can also be grown in containers—large pots, troughs and hanging baskets—or in the ground.

Step-by-Step

HOW TO PLANT STRAWBERRIES

1 Dig over the ground thoroughly. Mix in compost or manure. Dig a hole around twice the width and the same depth as the root ball of the plant. For a bare-rooted plant, create a small mound of soil in the centre of the hole.

2 Spread the roots over the mound so the crown of the plant will be just above the finished ground level. If you are planting out a potted strawberry, remove the pot, then gently run your fingers around the root ball to tease out the roots.

3 Place the plant in the hole so the level of the potting mix is at ground level.

4 Back-fill with soil. Apply controlled-release fertiliser around the plant. Water in, mulch with straw or sugarcane, and water again.

CHAPTER 5

Urban organic

Why do I need to read this chapter?

Working with small spaces

Even if you have only a small space to allocate to a garden you can use that space for growing a productive plant. Provided you have a sunny aspect, fruit trees, vegetables and herbs can be grown in small areas in the ground, in raised garden beds, or in containers if there's no access to soil. And this can all be achieved following organic principles.

The key to success is selecting compact varieties and managing their growth so the plants are trained to use the small space that's available. Also consider substituting a productive plant for an ornamental feature tree, hedge or screen planting. For example, the tea camellia (*Camellia sinensis*) can be grown as an evergreen hedge anywhere camellias are grown and its new shoots harvested for tea. An apple, plum, citrus or even a nut tree can be planted as a feature tree. Mangos, avocados or macadamias provide a shady canopy in a tropical garden. Fruiting trees and vines can also be trained over pergolas for shade.

Look beyond your boundaries too. The space between footpath and front fence, or the nature strip, may be available for productive planting. Check the soil for pollutants and consult your local council first, though.

Remember that a plant's basic need for sunshine must always be fulfilled.

Even when space is tight, you still need a brightly lit spot that receives at least four to six hours of sunshine, preferably from early morning. More sunshine is even better.

Getting started

Although vegetables and fruit trees are normally grown in the back garden, the sunniest part of a small property may be at the front or the side of the house. In built-up areas a garden may be overshadowed by surrounding buildings or structures such as walls, so take all these factors into account when assessing the amount of sun your proposed gardening site receives.

You may be able to access more light by elevating the plants in a raised garden bed or a vertical garden, by concentrating on growing vines that will climb into a better lit area on a trellis or side wall, or by erecting a climbing frame such as a tripod.

Bamboo canes are ideal for making a smaller, temporary tripod; stakes are more permanent. You can use as many canes as you like. For beans, use around eight or ten, with one or two bean seeds to each cane. For a single climbing plant, three canes may be enough support. Push each cane into the ground so it's at least 10 cm deep and well anchored, using a hammer or mallet to knock them in firmly. Collect the canes together at the top, and about 15 cm down from the tips, tie them together with strong twine.

Productive fruiting vines include passionfruit, kiwifruit and grapes. Productive vegetable vines include climbing beans, peas and cucumbers. Plants that trail across the ground, such as pumpkin and sweet potato, can also be trained to grow vertically to make the most of a small area.

It is also possible to grow cascading plants such as thyme or strawberries in hanging baskets or at the edges of large containers or raised beds.

RIGHT Climbing plants such as beans make good use of sunny walls or can be trained to grow up decorative trellises. Use the space around them for herbs or other vegetables. To make your productive garden look good, select varieties that have ornamental flowers, fruit or leaves as well as being edible.

Warning In inner-city areas, particularly in land adjacent to roadways, where renovations have occurred or that has previously been an industrial site, always have your soil checked for contaminants before you begin to grow edible plants. For more on this see Chapter 1, 'What was here before', page 14.

Ideas for managing plants in small spaces

Although a large number of dwarf fruit trees are now available—mostly selected varieties grown on dwarf rootstock—gardening techniques can be used to manage ordinary-sized fruiting plants in small spaces.

Pruning

Regular pruning or training can be used to manage productive trees and shrubs in a small area, for example, by pruning them after harvest to keep them compact. Fruit trees that have outgrown their space can be pruned hard to reduce size and spread. As well as making the tree fit the space, hard pruning to lower the tree's height makes harvesting and pest management easier.

Espalier

Trees, shrubs and vines can be grown into a flat, vertical shape against a wall or fence by regular pruning and tying their branches to wires or a trellis. Plants trained in this way into horizontal layers or fans are said to be espaliered. Plants suited to espalier include citrus (especially lemons), apples and pears. Fruiting vines can also be managed as an espalier. For tips on how to espalier plants see 'How to espalier a fruit tree', opposite.

Topiary

This is another pruning technique used to manage the size and shape of a plant. While the word 'topiary' may conjure up visions of quirky animal shapes, the simplest of all topiaries is the lollipop shape—a ball of green on a straight stem. Evergreen trees are best suited to topiary and particularly successful productive choices are bay, cumquat and lillypilly. Cutting fruiting plants into topiaries will reduce fruiting if it is done before fruit matures, so do it after harvesting is over.

Multi-planting

To maximise the number of fruit trees in a small garden, plant two or three related plants in one growing hole—such as two plums or two pear trees. This technique allows you to grow varieties that can help to pollinate each other and provide longer cropping. Root competition reduces overall size.

Multi-grafting

Another option for cross-pollination and adding variety to a small garden is to grow fruit trees that have several different varieties grafted onto the one compatible rootstock. Citrus, stone and pome fruits are all available commercially as multi-grafts. The number of varieties grafted to one rootstock can range from two to five. Generally, the more varieties the more difficult it is to manage the tree's health and vigour, as in most cases one variety will dominate the others. Prune to keep all varieties roughly the same size to avoid having one take over.

ABOVE Productive plants, such as this bay, can be used as low hedges or borders, or trained as standards to add a layer of productive planting to a small space.

Dwarf hedges

Dwarf hedges can range from low hedges referred to as 'step-over' hedges to privacy screens or garden dividers 3 m or more high. The height of the hedge is determined by the rootstock if you are growing a dwarf, grafted variety such as an apple, or by the height of the selected variety. A miniature apple hedge can be as little as 30 cm high, while a hedge of dwarf avocados may grow 2.5 m tall, which is still a lot smaller than a mature avocado.

Step-by-Step

HOW TO ESPALIER A FRUIT TREE

When choosing a fruit tree to espalier, select one that has a straight stem and most of its branches growing in one plane.

1 Plant the tree close to the base of a trellis, fence or wall. Prune off any branches that are growing back towards the trellis.

2 Tie the main trunk to the trellis with twist ties, strips of pantihose, budding tape or strong twine.

3 Cut off any branches that are growing forwards, but keep the ones growing to each side.

4 Tie the branches on each side to the trellis. Pull them down to as near horizontal as the branches will allow without snapping. If the branch is difficult to bend into the desired position, bend it in stages over a few months.

5 As the plant grows, regularly check and adjust the ties so they don't cut into the bark. Also check the area behind the branches as this is a place that can harbour pests such as snails, mealy bug and scale.

6 Espalier plants can be trained in many interesting ornamental and decorative patterns including fans so the stem and branches add to the look and feel of the garden, as well as providing future flowers and fruits.

Step-by-Step

HOW TO TURN AN OLIVE OIL TIN INTO A PLANTER

1 Carefully remove the lid of the olive oil tin with a can opener.

2 For drainage, punch three holes in the base of the tin with a large nail.

3 Half-fill the tin with organic potting mix.

4 Place the plant in the tin and back-fill with potting mix. Water well.

Container growing

Many different types of containers can be used to grow fruit, vegetables and herbs in small spaces or difficult situations, ranging from pots to recycled olive or vegetable oil tins. As a rule of thumb, always use the largest container you can, matching it to root ball size. Make sure it is stable.

Large black plastic pots, half wine barrels, large terracotta or glazed pots or recycled containers such as a washing-machine drum or a copper are all large enough to contain a dwarf fruit tree.

Containers at least 40 cm across, and 40 cm deep, are needed for fruit trees, large tomato plants and sweet potatoes.

Leafy vegetables, whose root systems are smaller, can be grown in window boxes, troughs or in individual recycled containers such as old tin cans. Leafy herbs such as basil or mint can look ornamental and will grow well in old olive oil containers, as do strawberries.

However, not all vegies can be squeezed into small pots. When selecting a container for root vegetables take into account root depth. Carrots,

Tip Do not use crocks in the base of pots that are to be filled with potting mix. Rather than improve drainage, crocks can create a raised watertable in the base of a pot that will adversely affect plant growth.

Tip For success with carrots in small containers or troughs, look for mini varieties that have small roots or mature early, such as 'Early Baby', which is ready to harvest at just 4 cm in length.

potatoes, turnips and sweet potatoes need ample space to form roots. A full-sized carrot such as 'Manchester Table' can grow a root that's 20 cm long. For this plant to grow successfully, the container would need to be at least 30–40 cm deep. Potatoes too need lots of root space, so plant in bags or containers that are at least 90 cm deep.

Avoid overplanting. Plan for the maximum size of a productive plant by restricting the numbers grown in individual containers. If the plant is given the maximum growing space then it will grow strongly, have fewer pest and disease problems, and have a better yield.

Containerised fruit trees and vegies need good drainage. Achieve this with adequate drainage holes in the base, raising it above ground level on bricks or pot feet, and filling with a good quality organic potting mix (or a mixture of potting mix and loam or compost).

RIGHT Productive plants can be used for their appearance as well as their edible crop. This row of potted lemon trees makes an impressive sight in terracotta pots.

Ongoing care

Once you have your potted vegie garden planted, its growth and productivity comes down to ongoing care, including adequate water, regular nourishment and protection from extremes of heat and cold.

Potted plants, particularly leafy vegetables, should be checked daily, and more frequently when the weather is hot or windy, as their water needs rise.

So what do we mean by 'checked'? Feel the soil to see if it is moist or dry, observe the plant for signs of wilting, pests or disease, and harvest anything that's ready to pick. Daily care and attention in this way reduces the chance of major problems occurring.

Watering

In most instances potted plants need daily watering. Allowing productive plants to dry out affects the quality of their produce and their life cycle.

If leafy vegetables dry out they are likely to switch from leafy growth to flowering, a process called bolting. When this occurs, the leaves often become tough and bitter as the plant is on its way to seeding and dying. Lettuce is prone to bolting if it becomes water-stressed, as are the leafy herbs rocket and coriander.

Fruiting vegetables such as tomatoes and capsicum that become water-stressed may drop fruit, the fruit may split or scald or they may stop fruiting.

The effect of drying out on fruit trees, particularly citrus, is similar, with fruit and often foliage being discarded.

Erratic watering—that is, allowing plants to dry out then compensating by over-watering—can also cause problems. Fruit may split or suffer from

nutrient deficiency (see 'Blossom end rot' in Chapter 11, page 174).

As well, plants that are subject to water stress are more likely to attract pests or succumb to disease problems. None of these results is ideal, so get into the habit of checking pots every day to see if they require water.

Nourishment

Although there is a certain amount of nourishment in potting mixes, particularly if fertiliser was added at planting time, the nutrients may be expended quite quickly. They are leached from the soil through watering and also taken up by the plant to fuel rapid growth.

To keep potted plants growing evenly requires additional fertiliser. The amount and frequency of fertiliser application depends on the plant you are growing. As a rule of thumb, plants use fertiliser when they are actively growing and also to stimulate flower and fruit production.

Vegetables that are being grown for their leaves, such as lettuce, salad and

FAR LEFT Use your finger to check the moisture of the soil below the mulch. Soil should be moist. If the soil feels dry and especially if plants are wilting, add water.

LEFT To keep herbs growing strongly never let them dry out. In hot weather, this may mean daily watering—in the morning is best. Herbs also respond to regular feeding, so apply liquid fertiliser once a week.

Don't contain me

While there are many productive plants for containers, some plants are not suited to container life however large their container. Large, bushy plants can become unstable in a pot and may be blown over. Plants with large underground tubers or roots, such as full-sized carrots and parsnips, and large and vigorous plants like sweetcorn and giant sunflowers, are generally unsuited to container growing.

Consider growing these plants in a raised garden bed or put your name down for a plot in a community garden.

Fruiting plants that do not do well in containers include kiwifruit, passionfruit, grapevines, berry plants including raspberry and blackberry, and the fruit salad plant (*Monstera deliciosa*). Figs and olives, along with citrus trees that have not been grafted on to dwarf rootstock, are not suited to long-term life in a container but may prosper for a few years.

Asian greens, cabbage, rocket, spinach, rhubarb, silverbeet and most herbs, need regular applications of fertiliser that's high in nitrogen or that has been specially formulated for leafy plants. Fertilisers can be applied as pellets to the surface or watered on as a liquid.

Liquid feeds can be applied to actively growing vegetables every seven to 14 days. Alternatively, apply a slow-release fertiliser. Slow-release products reduce fertiliser loss through leaching.

If you are making your own liquid compost or using diluted worm wee from your worm farm, adjust the strength and rate of application by observing plant growth. If the plants become very lush with leaves that are very dark green and larger than normal, you may be providing too much fertiliser and need to reduce the frequency of application.

If, on the other hand, the plants are not thriving, have pale green or yellow leaves or leaves that appear smaller than usual, apply a pelletised or slow-release fertiliser, increase the rate and strength of the liquid fertiliser you are using, or switch to a different type of fertiliser.

Also check water is soaking into the root ball and not simply running through the potting mix and flowing out from the base. This happens if potting mix has dried out and become water-repellent or if the potting mix has shrunk from the side of the pot. Plants that are not getting enough water are unable to take up nutrients from the soil, so may not thrive.

In these situations, apply an organic soil-wetting agent or dunk the entire pot into a large container of water until the potting mix and the plant are rehydrated.

Position

Plants in pots are more likely to be affected by extremes in weather than the same plants growing in the ground. Pots become hotter in summer and colder in winter. If the root ball is exposed to too much heat or cold the plant's growth may slow or it can die.

Potted plants are also likely to be blown over in wind, particularly if the top of the plant is larger than its base, or very bushy, or if it has become dried out.

To moderate the effects of weather, position potted plants in a sheltered spot. Cluster pots together in summer so they shade each other, or stand a lone pot in a second container to keep it cool. Add mulch to the surface of the potting mix to keep the temperature in the pot lower on a hot day.

When it is very cold, pots can crack or the plants themselves can be damaged, so move them to a warm spot. Protect pots with a wrapping of hessian or plastic.

Step-by-Step

HOW TO PLANT A POTTED HERB GARDEN

1 Fill half the pot with organic potting mix.

2 Position the tallest plant in the middle. Here we've used rosemary. Add more potting mix to anchor the centre plant, and to raise the soil level until it's at the right height for the smaller plants.

3 Adjust the positions of the smaller herbs around the edge of the pot until they look right.

4 Back-fill with potting mix, firming it down into all the gaps between each plant and the pot.

5 Mulch around the plants with lucerne or sugarcane.

6 Water well. Water every day or so as herbs do best if they are kept moist. Once a week apply a liquid fertiliser while watering to keep them growing strongly.

HINT *Put the pot into its final spot before you plant it up. It will be too heavy to move otherwise. The best spot is in full sun and close to the kitchen door so it's easy to access any time you're cooking.*

Compact fruit trees

For a small space, select dwarf or compact forms of fruiting plants to make the most of the area. These may be naturally compact varieties such as Ballerina series apples, 'Pixzee' peaches or 'Nectazee' nectarines, or full-size varieties that have been grafted onto dwarf rootstock.

A number of citrus fruits—grapefruit, calamondin, lime, mandarin, oranges and the 'Lemonade' lemon—are grafted on to a dwarfing rootstock called 'Flying Dragon' which modifies the size of the top growth to allow the tree to fit easily into a small garden. The fruit, however, is still full size. Expect these trees to be half the size of the same cultivar grown on ordinary citrus understock such as 'Trifoliata'.

Dwarfing rootstocks are available for lots of other fruiting plants, including mangos, avocados, apples and cherries. These plants are usually around 50 per cent of their normal size, but produce full-sized fruit.

There are many small-growing varieties for small spaces. For a full list, see 'Small packages' on page 73.

However, it isn't always necessary to go down the track of locating dwarf tree varieties to grow your own fruit in a small space. There are also fruiting vines, shrubs and perennials.

If you haven't got much room in the garden, consider growing strawberries, a hedge of raspberries or bramble berries, or a couple of blueberry plants. Use vertical space or a pergola to train climbing fruit plants such as passionfruit, grapevine or kiwifruit. Even a large sprawling choko vine can be grown in a small space by encouraging it to climb along a fence or over a wall.

RIGHT Dwarf apple trees are ideal to plant in small gardens as they can be readily trained as espaliers along wires or a fence.

Filling a large container

When you are growing a productive plant such as a fruit tree in a container make it a large container so that you provide a good growing environment for the plant's root system. As a large, planted-up pot can be extremely heavy and difficult to lift, the pot should be moved into position before planting. The weight also increases after watering.

To extend time before repotting is needed, add garden loam, coarse sand or a mix of compost and aged manure to the potting mix before planting. Around 10 per cent loam, sand, compost or manure by volume, and 90 per cent potting mix, slows down the process of slumping that occurs in potting mix as nourishment is taken up by the growing plant.

Compact vegetables

Along with the increasing number of dwarf vegetables now available, vegies such as shallots, softhearted lettuce, English spinach and chillies are ideal for growing in small spaces.

Most herbs are also space misers. Giving particularly good value for the space they occupy are basil, chives, mint, parsley and thyme.

Climbing vegetables such as peas, beans and cucumbers, along with some pumpkins such as butternut, can be trained on a tripod or against a climbing frame. While these are not dwarf vegetables, they do make excellent use of small spaces.

As well as considering the size of the crop, assess how long the variety will take up space in your garden until it is ready to harvest. Fast-maturing vegetables allow more crops to be grown in succession. Slow-maturing vegetables, even if small, occupy valuable garden space over many weeks.

Compact forms also allow for closer spacing of crops and of rows. Look at the spacing between plants as well as the height of the plant to get an idea of how much space is needed to grow a worthwhile crop.

Organic suppliers

While it may not always be possible to source dwarf fruiting plants from organic producers, a number of dwarf vegetable varieties are commonly available from organic seed suppliers. Many traditional seed companies also produce organic seeds.

If you can't find an organic supplier, it's best to remove all potting mix from the roots before planting. Take the plant from its pot, hose or shake off all the potting mix. Plant with care so that the roots are surrounded by soil.

Small packages

Here is a selection of fruit and vegetables suited to small spaces.

MINI-ORCHARDS

Small or dwarf fruit trees, 1–2 m high, to grow as a mini orchard or even in large containers on a sunny patio.

Fruit	Small cultivar	Comment
apple	'Tango'	Ballerina series
	'Waltz'	Ballerina series
avocado	'Secondo'	normal-sized fruit
	'Wurtz'	normal-sized fruit
crabapple	'Maypole'	Ballerina series
lemon	'Meyer'	thin skins
	'Lots 'a' Lemons'	productive even while young
mandarin	dwarf form	look for 'Flying Dragon' rootstock
mango	'Irwin'	dwarf tree, anthracnose resistant
	'Palmer'	dwarf rootstock
mulberry	'Dwarf Black'	dwarf rootstock
nectarine	'Nectazee'	small variety, normal-sized fruit
peach	'Pixzee'	small variety, normal-sized fruit

MINI VEGETABLES

Vegetables also come in small packages.
Here are some great little offerings for pots or small spaces.

Name	Variety	Maturity/comment
beans	'Plazza' and many other dwarf varieties	6 weeks/1 m tall, long pods
beetroot	'Baby'	6–7 weeks/small globes
broad beans	'Dwarf Prolific', 'Coles Dwarf'	12–14 weeks/1 m tall, small pods
cabbage	'Earliball'	8–10 weeks/compact 1–2 kg heads
carrot	'Baby'	10–12 weeks/4 cm roots
cauliflower	'Mini'	10–14 weeks/10 cm curd
peas	'Earlicrop Massey'	12–14 weeks/dwarf plant
pumpkin	'Little Dumpling'	9–10 weeks/compact plant
tomato	'Tiny Tim'	10–12 weeks/doesn't require staking

FAR LEFT Make the most of empty spaces to grow a quick crop of softhearted lettuce plants. These lettuce are being popped in under a teepee support for a crop of peas.

LEFT Climbing plants such as peas (shown) and beans are highly productive vegie choices for small spaces. They can be grown in beds or containers and trained on a trellis or stakes.

Warning Don't assume that all vegetable plants labelled 'dwarf' or 'mini' necessarily indicate a small plant. Some plants produce smaller than normal fruit—but the plant itself may not be compact. Cherry tomatoes are small but they are produced on large, sprawling vines that need to be staked and given adequate garden space. On the other hand, while small-fruited varieties are not always compact, they often crop more quickly than larger fruited varieties and can make better pot plants.

Waste

One of the dilemmas when gardening in a small space is what to do with waste from the garden and the kitchen. In even the smallest of spaces, however, it is possible to have a compost bin or a worm farm (or both) to turn waste into organic nutrients for your garden.

The key to success is to chop up all materials before they go into the compost bin or worm farm. Scraps can even be put through the blender to speed up decomposition. This approach, when combined with regular aeration of the compost bin's contents, ensures that all material composts quickly so they break down fast.

You can also add used potting mix and chopped prunings to your compost bin to help recycle waste from the garden and reduce the amount you send to landfill through your garbage system. Put prunings through a mulching machine or chop them up finely with secateurs or pruning shears.

Step-by-Step

HOW TO SET UP A WORM FARM KIT

1 Fill a bucket with water and place the bedding block into it. As the block expands, crumble it up. Lay cardboard in the base of the worm farm. Spread the expanded block over the top.

2 You need around 1000 compost worms to start a worm farm. Gently spread the worms over the bedding.

3 Cover with a worm blanket and put on the lid. There are specially designed blankets available, or you can use newspaper or hessian bags. Leave the worms to settle in for a couple of days.

4 You can feed worms most kitchen scraps, but avoid meat, large quantities of citrus, onion or dairy foods. Always place the food under the blanket. Never cover more than half the surface with food at a time, and make the layer of food about 2 cm thick.

Use the homemade compost to mulch garden beds or pots, and as a soil improver to dig in before new plantings are made. Compost can also be added to potting mix or applied as mulch.

In apartments with a communal garden where it is not possible to have a compost heap, consider burying your scraps, or using a Bokashi bucket.

The Bokashi system allows for the easy disposal and decomposition of kitchen scraps in a sealed bucket. Once the bucket is filled it must be emptied into a pit in the garden. If there's no suitable space in your garden, you may be able to donate the composted waste to your local community or school garden (see 'Communal options', page 77).

BELOW Worm farms need moisture too. This child's watering can is an easy way to apply a small amount of moisture. Worms also produce liquid. Drained from the farm it is diluted and applied to potted plants as liquid fertiliser.

Tip Seed can be sprouted in a seed tray using seed-raising mix, or even on layers of paper towel. Sow thickly. When the seed has sprouted it can be harvested simply by snipping with kitchen scissors. These crops are known as microgreens.

Indoor growing

Even if your garden is restricted to a sunny windowsill it is still possible to grow some types of productive plants such as herbs. For success, though, they will need at least four to six hours of sunlight each day.

When all else fails, you can sprout seed, even in a poorly lit space. As well as being easy to grow, sprouts are rich in vitamins and high in fibre, and provide a nutritious addition to salads, sandwiches and stir-fries.

All you need to sprout seed are clean jars or plastic containers, a piece of mesh (such as muslin, stocking or flyscreen), a rubber band, seeds and water (see Step-by-Step, below). The ideal place to sprout seed in most homes is next to the kitchen sink where it's well lit and there's quick access to water and a drain.

Organic sprouting seed mixes are available from seed outlets or by mail order, or you can buy mung bean, alfalfa, pea, lentil or sunflower seeds and make your own sprout mixes.

Step-by-Step

HOW TO SPROUT SEEDS

1 Put a small amount of your selected seed in a jar with some warm water to soak overnight. This initiates germination.

2 Cover the mouth of the jar with a piece of mesh, secure it with a rubber band, and pour out the water.

3 Several times a day fill the jar with water and then allow it to drain out. This flushes the seed. Make sure the water drains away completely to prevent the seed rotting or harmful bacteria developing. To further reduce the risk, lay the jar on its side at an angle so any excess dampness drains away.

4 When the first pair of true leaves develops it's time to harvest your sprouts. As sprouts quickly become bitter, only germinate small amounts of seed at a time.

HINT *When your sprouts are ready to harvest, you can store them in a sealed container or ziplock bag in the fridge. This should keep them fresh for at least a week. Dry sprouts last the longest so allow them to drain for 5–10 hours before popping them in the fridge—simply turn the jar upside down so the water can drain out of the mesh covering.*

Communal options

Community gardens are spaces in a neighbourhood where land is made available for growing vegetables. They are normally overseen by the local council and administered by a committee made up of plot holders and local council representatives. There is usually a small annual fee involved. Extra charges for water may also be made in some areas.

If your garden is too small or too shaded to grow your own plants, ask your local council about the availability of community gardens. There may be a waiting list for a plot.

Most community gardens have sets of rules and regulations which cover the types of structures that can be erected, the types of plants that can be grown, the chemicals that may be used (most follow organic growing principles) and the hours the garden may be accessed. Some provide facilities and equipment on a share basis.

Many schools have a vegetable garden for their students to grow crops. As with community gardens, most of these are managed following organic growing methods. Parent and local community involvement is generally welcomed, so enquire at schools in your neighbourhood if you would like to assist in a school garden.

HOW TO MAKE INSTANT COMPOST

If you don't have room for a compost bin in your garden, you can make use of some kitchen scraps by making instant compost.

1 Dig a hole around 30 cm deep. Don't dig too close to shrubs as you don't want to disturb their roots.

2 Chop up the vegie scraps. The smaller the pieces, the more quickly they will break down. Tip the scraps into the hole.

3 Back-fill the hole with the dug-out soil, then water.

RIGHT School gardens welcome parent and community support to grow organic produce.

CHAPTER 6

Planning crops

Why do I need to read this chapter?

- 🖐 PAGE 80 To find out how to plan crops from your
  productive garden and avoid gluts.

- 🖐 PAGE 84 For information about crop rotation and
  how it helps keep your garden disease free.

- 🖐 PAGE 88 To discover planting information to get
  you growing.

Well planned and planted

The aim of this chapter is to provide information on how to plan and regulate production in your vegetable garden. Planning is vital to making the best use of space and to the health of your crops. It is particularly important for organic gardeners as good planning through sensible crop rotation also reduces pest and disease problems and makes the best use of soil nutrients.

If your objective for growing vegetables in your backyard is to reduce your impact on the planet and enjoy fresh, seasonal produce, you also need to get a handle on what is grown in which season, and when seeds or seedlings should be planted to best suit their seasonal requirements.

Keeping a record

To help manage your vegie garden, keep a record of what you planted and when it was planted, along with when a crop was harvested and the size of the yield. This record can take the form of labels in the garden, a list in a notebook or a spreadsheet on your computer. Also make a habit of keeping a note of which varieties you have grown so you can grow the successful ones again.

Getting started

When you are starting out growing vegetables or planting fruit trees your first thought is to plant everything. But if you visit a nursery or shop online without a plan you may well find yourself laden down (or inundated) with more plants than you know what to do with. You may also have purchased plants that don't grow well in your area or shouldn't be planted at that particular time of the year.

Without dampening your enthusiasm for getting started, take a little time to plan your garden before you start shopping for plants.

The basic things to decide on are: what things you like to eat; what types of vegetables suit your garden; and what you've got the room and the resources to grow. Within this broad outline, match what you *can* grow with what you *want* to grow.

The next step is to divide your crops into seasons and quantities. Check you've planned your crops to have something to harvest all year.

Gardening is all about looking ahead. So, from your list of potential crops and the season in which they are harvested, work back through the life cycle of each plant to see when they should be planted. As a general guide, vegetables are planted one to two seasons before they are harvested.

Quantities

Next, work out quantities. How many plants do you need to grow to produce the amounts you want to eat?

If you are gardening to supplement your vegetable needs rather than to supply everything you are planning on eating, getting quantities right is not critical. If your aim is to be self-sufficient, however, then the amounts you produce and their timing and length of cropping become all-important.

LEFT Cabbages can take four months to reach harvest, but silverbeet can be picked as required as soon as the outer leaves are well developed.

BELOW Beetroot has delicious red roots but its leaves can be harvested too to add to salads or stir-fry dishes. Pick them as they grow.

Sorting storage

As well as deciding what to plant, you also need to plan how you are going to preserve your crops, as not everything can be eaten fresh. For example, if you plan to freeze some of your produce, you need to have a freezer that's large enough. If you plan to bottle and preserve what can't be frozen or eaten fresh from the garden, you need containers and secure storage space to hold your preserves.

Remember, however, that even a well-devised and finely calculated growing plan is just that, a plan. Crops may fail or be unexpectedly abundant and the end quantities may be very different from what you anticipated.

Finally, don't expect to get things right from the very beginning. It may take several seasons to understand the production and timing of various crops in your local soil and climate. Eventually though you will have the experience to know how much to plant and grow.

Gauge your harvest

To estimate how many plants will provide a harvest sufficient for your needs, make some quick calculations. While exact quantities will vary depending on growing conditions and the variety you have chosen, you can generally find out from seed suppliers how much crop each plant is likely to produce. For a rough guide of the amount that's harvested from some of the most popular backyard crops, see our chart 'How much?', right.

Use figures provided as a guide to the number of plants you'll need to feed your family. To do this, compare the quantity that a single plant produces with the amount you think your family may consume. This not only helps you to work out how many of each plant you'll need to grow, it will also tell you how big your vegetable garden will have to be to fit everything in.

BELOW Pick outer leaves of softhearted lettuce as you need them so the main plant keeps growing.

How much?

Here's a guide to the productivity of a number of commonly grown vegetables. Remember that different varieties of the same vegetable have different yields. Growing different varieties and staggering planting times will allow you to maximise your harvest.

Vegetable	Yield (per plant, unless stated otherwise)
Asian greens	500 g–1.5 kg
beans	100–500 g
beetroot	400 g
broad beans	300–400 g
broccoli	250–750 g
cabbage	1.5–3.5 kg
capsicum	1–4 kg
carrot	200 g
cauliflower	500 g–2.5 kg
cucumber	5–30 kg
eggplant	5–30 kg
lettuce	100–500 g
onion	30–120 g
peas	100 g
potato	1–4 kg
pumpkin	3–30 kg
silverbeet	2 kg per metre
snow peas	1–5 kg per metre
spinach (English)	2 kg per metre
spring onion	1 kg per metre
sweet corn	10 cobs
tomato	2–8 kg
zucchini	1–4 kg

Avoiding a glut

While you want to make sure you are growing enough of each vegetable, what you don't want is to have vast quantities of a particular vegetable to eat all at once. Having too much of any type of crop is a glut. For the home gardener, it is always better to have crops arranged to mature at different times so that they are in season for as long as possible.

One way to achieve this is to plant small amounts every few weeks. This is known as making successive plantings. As well, plant several different varieties of a vegetable, including some that crop early and others that extend the season by cropping later. The times of maturity are often indicated by varietal names or descriptions, with terms such as 'early' and 'late' used to describe cropping times.

The selection of early and late maturing varieties is particularly important when you are planning an orchard for fruit production. With care it is possible to have a succession of fruit produced from the beginning to the end of the overall harvest season.

BELOW Fast-growing crops can be added in space left by harvested plants to keep space being productive. Here beetroot has replaced some of the leeks that have been harvested.

BELOW Peas quickly fill any spare corners and begin to harvest in a matter of weeks. Harvest regularly taking only what is needed.

Crop rotation

Crop rotation can be a difficult concept to get your head around, but once you've grasped the principles it is easy to implement. The basic premise is that each vegetable carries its own baggage in the form of associated pest and disease problems. Different vegetables also use different types of nutrients and some even return nutrients to the soil.

By growing a particular crop in a different part of the garden each season, you reduce the likelihood of a build-up of pests and diseases that are specific to that vegie, and you avoid depleting the soil of the nutrients it needs.

There is a complication, however, and it comes about because some vegetables are very closely related to others. Related vegetables can share a predisposition to certain pests and diseases and may also draw upon the same nutrients in the soil.

These related plants have been identified by botanists and grouped together in plant families. They are usually grouped on the basis of similarities in their flower type but the relationship may not be apparent on casual observation, particularly where different parts of the plant are eaten.

For example, tomatoes and potatoes are closely related to each other, as are carrots and parsley. Potatoes and tomatoes belong in the Solanaceae family, carrots and parsley are in the Asteraceae family.

To see which vegetable plants fall into the same family groups, see 'All in the family' on page 86.

So, for successful crop rotation, it is vital not only to move vegies to a different spot each season, but also not to plant close relatives in the same place.

To simplify this moving around, grow vegetables in dedicated beds, planting each bed with related plants. Then grow an unrelated group of plants in each bed in the next season. Keep moving in an ordered way from one bed to the next so that a vegetable eventually returns to the original bed in four to six seasons (depending on how many beds you have).

To make the most of the growing conditions left behind after each crop has finished, it makes sense to replant the bed with a compatible crop. There are a number of crop rotation planting plans which can be adjusted to suit what you are growing. One of the most basic forms of crop rotation is to replace summer crops with winter vegetables, as these tend to be in different family groups. For a more complex rotation system, which allows for a break of four years before a crop returns to its original bed, see our plan, right.

LEFT By growing related plants together in beds you can more easily implement crop rotation.

RIGHT Grow plants of the same family in a different bed at each planting so that it is four years before they are planted in Bed 1 again.

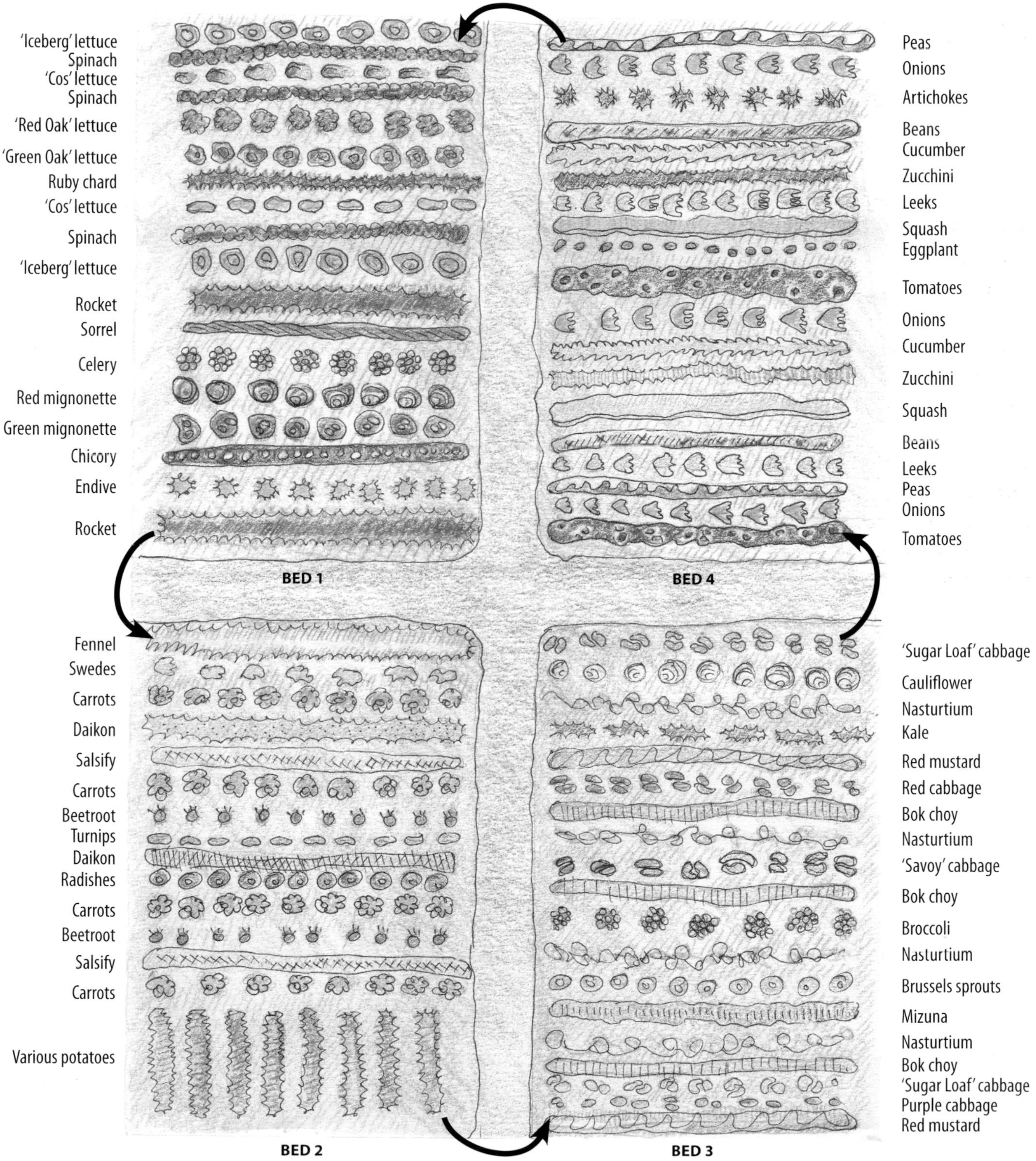

BED 1

'Iceberg' lettuce
Spinach
'Cos' lettuce
Spinach
'Red Oak' lettuce
'Green Oak' lettuce
Ruby chard
'Cos' lettuce
Spinach
'Iceberg' lettuce
Rocket
Sorrel
Celery
Red mignonette
Green mignonette
Chicory
Endive
Rocket

BED 4

Peas
Onions
Artichokes
Beans
Cucumber
Zucchini
Leeks
Squash
Eggplant
Tomatoes
Onions
Cucumber
Zucchini
Squash
Beans
Leeks
Peas
Onions
Tomatoes

BED 2

Fennel
Swedes
Carrots
Daikon
Salsify
Carrots
Beetroot
Turnips
Daikon
Radishes
Carrots
Beetroot
Salsify
Carrots
Various potatoes

BED 3

'Sugar Loaf' cabbage
Cauliflower
Nasturtium
Kale
Red mustard
Red cabbage
Bok choy
Nasturtium
'Savoy' cabbage
Bok choy
Broccoli
Nasturtium
Brussels sprouts
Mizuna
Nasturtium
Bok choy
'Sugar Loaf' cabbage
Purple cabbage
Red mustard

ALL IN THE FAMILY

Family	Common name	Vegetables
Amaryllidaceae	onion family	garlic, leek, onion, shallot
Asteraceae	carrot family	artichoke, carrot, celeriac, celery, coriander, endive, fennel, lettuce, parsley, parsnip
Brassicaceae	cabbage family, also called brassicas	bok choy, broccoli, brussels sprouts, cabbage, cauliflower, daikon, kale, kohl rabi, mustard, radish, swede, turnip, watercress
Chenopodiaceae	beet family	beetroot, chard, English spinach, silverbeet
Convolvulaceae	convolvulus family	sweet potato
Cucurbitaceae	pumpkin family, also called cucurbits	cucumber, gourd, melons, pumpkin, squash, zucchini
Fabaceae	pea family, also called legumes	beans, broad bean, lentils, peanuts, peas
Poaceae	grass family	sweetcorn
Malvaceae	hibiscus family	okra, rosella
Polygonaceae	rhubarb family	rhubarb, sorrel
Solanaceae	potato family	capsicum, chilli, eggplant, potato, tomato

Mutual benefit

Here are some of the nutritional and physical benefits obtained from crop rotation in the vegetable patch. Use these benefits to tailor your own crop rotation system. Leguminous plants, which are plants in the Fabaceae family such as peas and beans, add nitrogen to the soil as they grow.

This process is called fixing nitrogen in the soil. Following a crop of legumes with a leafy crop that likes lots of nitrogen (such as spinach or silverbeet) can reduce the need for added high-nitrogen fertiliser. Tall crops such as sweetcorn can be used to shelter smaller plants such as lettuce so it is good to plant a tall crop on the wind-exposed side of a crop that needs shelter.

Follow a crop that takes a lot of nitrogen from the soil, such as sweetcorn, with one that doesn't, such as carrots.

RIGHT Broad beans are part of the Fabaceae family, which also includes peas and peanuts.

FAR RIGHT Crop rotation systems work particularly well in large gardens with formal beds. In small areas, however, crops can be rotated using pots or foam boxes, remembering to avoid planting the same vegetable in the same potting mix from year to year.

Get growing

Planning crops also involves assessing how best to start the particular vegetable and herb growing. Most are vegies grown from seed, but some are grown from tubers. The seed may be direct sown, or planted into a seed tray or punnet and planted out when it has reached a manageable size.

When sowing seed, make sure it is sown evenly and not buried too deeply. Most seeds are sown at or near the soil surface and covered with a light dusting of fine soil or seed-raising mix. Some larger seeds are pressed more firmly into the ground.

If seeds are too thickly sown they are prone to diseases such as damping off at or just after germination. For tips on how to sow fine seed, see 'How to sow carrot seed' on page 90.

Where seeds are sown too close together they must be thinned out after germination so the plants are spaced at their recommended distances from each other. Thin seedlings while they are still small. Leave the strongest growing to reach maturity. Seedlings can be replanted elsewhere or eaten.

Step-by-Step

HOW TO TAKE CUTTINGS OF ROSEMARY

To increase your plant stock for free, propagation is the way to go. Many shrubs, such as rosemary, propagate well from semi-hardwood cuttings. These are stems that have just started to firm up, which means the base is quite hard while the tip is still flexible and growing. They are usually taken in mid to late summer.

1 Select a healthy shoot of the current season's growth. Take a cutting about 15–20 cm long, just above a stem node, with clean, sharp secateurs.

2 Trim the stem to 10–15 cm, cutting just below a stem joint. Cut off the soft tip.

3 Remove any side-shoots from the stem and the leaves from the lower half of the cutting.

4 Dip the base of the cutting in hormone rooting compound so that it has a thin but even coverage. Shake off the excess. Fill a 50–100 mm pot with propagating mix. Make a hole with a dibbler, or use a chopstick or a pencil. Insert the cutting so that the lowest leaves lie just above the surface. Firm the soil around the cutting. Water well.

HINT *Honey is also useful to promote root formation and can be used instead of a commercial rooting hormone. Simply dip the cut end of the cutting in honey.*

Rows should also be far enough apart to allow the plants to reach their mature size. These recommended spacings allow for the plant to grow to its full width without becoming engulfed by its neighbour. Plants that are too closely spaced may also fail to reach a good size and yield will be reduced.

Herbs can be grown from seed, division or cutting. Woody or shrubby herbs such as rosemary and lavender can readily grow from a cutting (see 'How to take cuttings of rosemary', left). Those that spread readily, such as mint, can be grown from a stem or root cutting or simply by dividing a large clump (see 'How to divide chives' on page 93).

RIGHT After germination thin seedlings to allow space for each plant to reach its full size. This produces stronger crops.

BELOW Some seeds are best raised in punnets or seed trays, rather than being direct sown.

Step-by-Step

HOW TO SOW CARROT SEED

To aid even spreading, fine seed such as carrot seed can be mixed with dry sand before it is sown.

1 Quarter-fill a jar with dry sand. Punch a hole in the lid with a nail. Pour in the seed, put on the lid and shake to mix.

2 Dig over the ground so that it has a fine, crumbly texture. Spread compost or manure, then dig it through until well combined. Make a furrow in the ground the length of the row and as deep as recommended for the seed. A rake or broom handle works well.

3 Pour the seed evenly along the row.

4 Back-fill the soil over the seeds. Water.

Seed raising

Seed raising takes longer and is more complicated than just buying seedlings from the nursery but it has lots of benefits. Growing your own plants from seed allows you to raise organic seed and to control the timing of your crop. If you sow heirloom or open-pollinated seed then you can also save your seed when your crop is finished by leaving some plants to flower and seed or by saving the best fruit from your harvest.

Heirloom and open-pollinated varieties that come true to type from seed are the best seeds for an organic gardener to grow. These varieties differ from many modern hybrid seeds, which do not come true (that is grow and crop

BELOW As your crops grow, keep an eye on those that are performing well. It may be worth saving their seed for replanting.

in the same way) when their seeds are collected and sown again. The progeny of hybrid seed may resemble one of the original plants used to create the hybrid rather than the plant you grow.

To store seed safely until it is time to plant again, keep it in a cool, dry spot in an airtight container. A glass jar with a screw lid, or a plastic container, is ideal for seed storage. Make sure it is thoroughly clean and dry to avoid any rot occurring while the seed is in storage. Clearly label and date the seed so you can keep track of it for replanting.

Sowing large seeds

Large seeds can be planted directly where they are to grow but often more than one seed is sown into the planting hole. When the seeds germinate the strongest seedling is kept and the weaker one removed or transplanted.

ABOVE Tomatoes can be grown from seed or by planting seedlings purchased from the nursery. Some tomatoes are also sold as grafted plants. When planting tomato seedlings or grafts, bury the tomato more deeply in the soil than it was growing in its pot for a stronger plant. Deep planting encourages more root growth from the stem. Not only is the plant more firmly rooted in the soil, it also has access to more soil moisture and nutrients via its larger root system.

LEFT Open-pollinated tomatoes such as cherry tomatoes can be easily grown from seed. Save the best fruit and remove the seed from the pulp. Wash and dry the seed before it is stored.

Step-by-Step

HOW TO DIVIDE CHIVES

Some plants are easily divided, which means that you can get many individual plants from just one clump. Plants to try include chives and spring onions. Next time you're at the nursery, look at the plants that can be easily split and buy the densest clump so you get the most plants for your money.

1   If you are splitting an existing clump, dig it up with a spade or trowel. Remove the container, if the plant is in a pot.

2   Divide the clump. You may need to use a spade to cut through the roots and separate the root ball into manageable pieces.

3   Continue to ease apart the roots until you've got small clumps of just a few plants.

4   Prepare the soil by adding compost or manure, then replant the little clumps in their new home. Water well, mulch and water again.

CHAPTER 7

Nutritious soils

Why do I need to read this chapter?

Creating the right soil

Get the soil right and you can grow just about anything. Good soil is truly the basis for any good garden, particularly a good organic garden. Not only does it support the roots of your plants, it also provides them with the water and nutrients they need to grow.

Often, however, the soil in a garden is far from perfect. It can be impossible to dig, hard to wet or, at the opposite end of the scale, soggy and hard to drain. It can be made of sticky clays that are impossible to dig when wet and crack apart when dry, or it may be sandy stuff that water just slips through, leaving behind parched plants. Soils may also be composed of shale or have lots of stones in among the soil particles.

Soils can also vary in different parts of the garden and can alter from the soil surface to the subsoil, the layer below the surface.

In areas that have been cleared, particularly land that was once orchards or that has been cleared of native vegetation to make way for subdivision, the topsoil may have been removed, leaving you with subsoil. In this case, your only options are to import new soil or to create your own with compost, manure and lots of mulch to help improve what you have.

What most plants need is a soil you find easy to dig. With such a soil it is a breeze to plant, and as the small plants grow their roots can penetrate the soil with ease.

Step-by-Step

HOW TO IDENTIFY SOIL TYPE

Soils are broadly classified as sand, loam or clay. If you are unsure about the type of soil in your garden there are various tests that can help you identify it.

1 Dig up a little soil and place it in a small container. Remove any plant material such as twigs or leaves.

2 Take a handful and work it until it is fine and crumbly. Remove any rocks or small stones. Add a little water.

3 Start kneading the soil in your hand until it forms a rough ball that is damp, but not wet. Add more water if necessary. Take note of how the soil feels. If it feels gritty, there is sand present. If it feels smooth and a bit sticky, and stains your hands, you have clay.

4 Place the ball in the palm of your hand and start pushing the soil over your forefinger with your thumb. If the 'ribbon' that forms is over 5 cm long, the soil has a high clay content. If you can't form a ribbon as it falls apart, the soil is very high in sand. If the ribbon is somewhere in between, you have loam.

BELOW Feeling your soil by rolling it in your hands can tell you a lot about its make-up. If it is firm but crumbly you have a good balance of clay and sand known as loam.

RIGHT Most soils have clearly defined layers known as horizons starting with the topsoil and moving down to parent rock. The best soil to cultivate will be the topsoil.

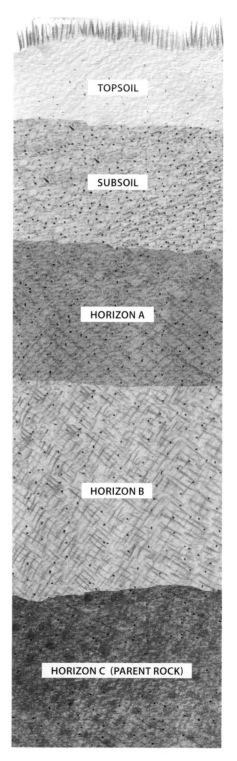

TOPSOIL

SUBSOIL

HORIZON A

HORIZON B

HORIZON C (PARENT ROCK)

Soil improvement

The good news is, no matter what type of soil you have in the garden, it can be turned into a soil that's easier to cultivate and that will provide better growing conditions for your plants. Although transforming soil usually means hard work and lots of perseverance, the rewards are long lasting.

In most instances, the easiest way to improve your soil is to add organic matter to it in the form of compost or rotted manure. This material can be dug in or simply spread over the surface as mulch. Top it with a layer of organic mulch such as chopped bark or green waste to stop weeds getting established.

Working in this way imitates nature. In a natural system, soils receive constant additions of nutrients from falling leaves, spent plants and animal manures that fall to the ground and which, through the action of organisms such as earthworms and microbes, break down to feed the soil.

Sandy soil

All sandy soils are made better for plant growth with extra organic matter. Incorporating organic matter adds nutrients and improves the sand's ability to hold moisture. In most cases sandy soils require continuous additions of organic matter to hold moisture and provide nutrients for plants.

Spread organic matter across the soil surface regularly, and dig in well-rotted organic matter prior to making any new plantings. Sandy soils may also become hydrophobic or water repellent, which means that water fails to soak into the soil. Plants in hydrophobic soils can wilt and die due to lack of water even when the garden is irrigated or it has rained.

To allow water to enter hydrophobic soil apply an organic soil-wetting agent and add compost. Adding the compost as slurry can help work nutrients quickly into the soil. It may be neccesary to repeat the application every six months.

Benefits of sandy soil
- Easy to dig
- Well drained
- Easy for plant roots to penetrate

RIGHT Homemade compost or well-rotted manures are excellent soil improvers to spread over soils and dig or fork in before planting.

Improving clay soil

Although a clay soil is very different from sand, the solution to making it a more user-friendly garden soil is the same as for sand—that is, to regularly dig organic matter into the clay and add it to the surface as mulch.

Some clay soils can also be improved by adding calcium sulphate, better known as gypsum but also sold as clay-breaker. When gypsum is added to clay soils it helps break down the clods and also releases minerals that are locked into the soil. Gypsum does not increase soil pH so it does not make alkaline soils more alkaline.

Gypsum is added to soils at a rate of 0.5–1 kg per square metre and is dug in well. Instructions on how much gypsum to apply are outlined on the product you buy so follow the recommended application rates.

Digging over a large garden area to establish garden beds can be backbreaking work so consider using a cultivator.

Benefits of clay soil

- Holds moisture
- Nutrient rich
- Readily transformed into a crumbly garden loam

RIGHT For large or hard-to-work areas of soil, use a powered cultivator to work the soil without breaking your back.

Step-by-Step

HOW TO ADD ORGANIC MATTER

1 Spread a good layer of compost (homemade or bought) or well-rotted manure over the surface of the soil. Around 5 cm is ideal.

2 Using a fork or spade, turn the organic matter through the soil so it's thoroughly mixed in.

3 Water well then apply mulch to reduce seed growth in the disturbed soil.

The Emerson Dispersion Test

Not all clay soils respond in the same
way to additives such as gypsum.
To find out whether a clay-based
soil will respond to gypsum you can
do a simple test called the Emerson
Dispersion Test.

All you need to do is take a small
lump of soil and leave it in a glass of
water overnight. A cloudy result, as
shown in the glass in the picture on the
far right means that if gypsum is added
to the soil it will help improve its
structure. Gypsum is best worked into
the soil before planting begins.

Reading the test results

- If the clay you added develops a
  halo and disperses into the water,
  it will respond to gypsum. The
  cloudier the water, the better the
  gypsum is likely to work.
- If the clay lump remains
  undissolved overnight (shown
  right, in the centre), gypsum is
  unlikely to help break down your
  soil. Instead, regularly add organic
  matter or create raised beds for your
  productive organic garden.
- If the lump falls apart (shown right,
  at the left), add organic matter to
  your soil to help bind it together.

RIGHT If a lump of clay soil makes water
in a glass cloudy (far right), adding gypsum
can improve it. If the soil lump fails to dissolve
or it forms a halo (centre), gypsum will make
little difference.

The role of fertiliser

Plants, particularly productive plants, need lots of input to grow. As well as water and sunlight, they need nutrients, most of which are obtained from the soil. As discussed in Chapter 1, the main nutrients required to allow plants to grow, flower and fruit are nitrogen, phosphorus and potassium (known collectively as NPK).

In manufactured fertilisers, as opposed to animal manures or compost, nitrogen is obtained from the atmosphere while potassium and phosphorus, both minerals, are mined.

Plants need NPK to grow, but the amounts needed vary depending on the plant and where it is in its life cycle. As a rule of thumb, nitrogen encourages leafy growth, phosphorus stimulates overall growth and development, while potassium assists with flowering. However, this is a very superficial dividing up of the way nutrients are used by plants. Most plants require different amounts of macronutrients at different stages of their development.

Macronutrients are found naturally in soils, but soils that are cropped repeatedly become depleted of their natural nutrients, which is why we need to add fertiliser.

Fertilisers contain varying ratios of NPK depending on their source or composition. On packaged fertilisers the amounts of NPK are generally shown as a ratio of one to the other. A packaged fertiliser which contains roughly equal proportions of the three macronutrients will be labelled 'complete' or 'balanced'.

Other fertilisers are tailored to suit specific growth needs. Lawn foods, for example, tend to have a higher proportion of nitrogen whereas citrus foods tend to have a higher proportion of phosphorus. Fertilisers formulated for Australian native plants are generally very low in phosphorus.

Plants require other nutrients too. These are the micronutrients. Calcium, magnesium, sulphur and iron also needed for growth are often included in manufactured fertilisers, or can be purchased separately, usually in chelated or readily dissolved form, to be watered over plants lacking some of these minor nutrients. Chelated iron, a form of liquid iron, will green up growth, while calcium can assist root development.

Plants also require trace elements. Of these, zinc, copper, manganese, boron and molybdenum are available in manufactured form to apply to soils or plants lacking trace elements. These are sold as 'rock minerals' or as trace elements and are worked into the soil at planting time.

> *Tip* After digging 200 g per square metre of gypsum into soil use the Emerson Dispersion Test (opposite) to see if it has worked. If the new sample settles to the bottom of the jar in five or ten minutes you've added enough gypsum. If it takes longer, add more gypsum to the soil then repeat the test.

SOURCES OF NPK

Complete manufactured fertilisers provide nitrogen, phosphorus and potassium to plants. The vital building blocks of growth are also derived from the following minerals and other products.

Product	Nutrients supplied
blood and bone	nitrogen, phosphorus, calcium and trace elements
compost	varies but most composts provide NPK and trace elements
eggshells	calcium
epsom salts	magnesium (not permitted by some organic certifiers)
gypsum	calcium, sulphur
manures	NPK (use aged or composted material)
rock phosphate	phosphorus, calcium
seaweed	potassium
wood ash	potassium and other minerals (can be extremely alkaline)

LEFT Old grass clippings are are mostly made of water, so they decompose quickly and release nitrogen and other nutrients, encouraging natural soil aeration.

Compost

Compost is the most popular fertiliser with organic gardeners—indeed, it is often described as 'garden gold'. Compost also acts as a soil conditioner and mulch, and increases the number of beneficial organisms in the soil. It can help combat soil-borne diseases, and creates a soil that's better able to retain soil moisture.

Compost is also popular because it is readily available and can be manufactured from waste materials generated in your own home and garden (see 'Five easy steps to great compost' in Chapter 2, page 23). In fact, an active compost heap is an indispensable part of an organic garden system as it allows nutrients to be retained and recycled within the garden. And it's free.

During the composting process organic matter is broken down by heat and microorganisms until it forms humus. Compost that is broken down at high temperatures is free of weed seeds and disease and particularly rich in organic matter such as humus.

The humus feeds the soil and also stimulates the growth of microorganisms that further benefit plant growth. But just because compost is homemade and natural doesn't mean that it can always supply all the nutrients your plants need. If plants are showing signs of nutrient deficiency, including stunted growth, add other fertilisers to your garden.

Adding fertiliser

Good use of fertilisers is as much about the right timing as the right product. Fertilisers have the biggest effect when plants are growing, forming buds or forming fruit.

With most plants, maximum growth occurs in spring as the soil and temperatures warm. Fertilisers that are applied in spring are taken up quickly to fuel growth.

Plants need fertiliser at other times of active growth, and at times of flower and fruit production. Additional applications are also needed after very wet conditions, such as a period of prolonged high rainfall, to replace what has been leached from the soil.

Warning Some composts can be highly alkaline, particularly if materials such as wood ash or lime have been added.

Plants lacking the nutrients needed for growth will exhibit signs of nutrient deficiency. They may become stunted, develop yellow leaves, drop flowers or fruit or even die. Over-fertilising can also cause problems, including toxicities and salt burn. Take particular care in applying any type of fertiliser that it does not come into direct contact with the plant's roots.

Soil pH can affect the plant's ability to absorb nutrients. When soil pH is either very acidic or very alkaline, many nutrients become unavailable, even if they are present naturally in the soil or have been added as fertiliser.

If your plants are exhibiting signs of nutrient deficiency, check soil pH before adding trace elements to the soil.

For example, lime-induced chlorosis, a yellowing of the leaves, is common in citrus and other acid-loving plants grown in very alkaline soils. The yellowing indicates the plant is lacking important micronutrients including iron.

However, unless the soil is acidified, for example by the addition of sulphur or aluminium, no amount of iron chelates will make iron available to the plant long term. Watering iron chelates and liquid nutrients over the foliage does green up foliage and alleviate chlorosis on a temporary basis. If the alkalinity is lowered, the problem will be remedied.

Note Some of the symptoms listed here can be caused by other environmental factors, such as pests, diseases, water stress or poor drainage, so it is important to assess what factors are affecting your plant before applying additional fertilisers.

Step-by-Step

HOW TO TEST pH

Soil pH is a measure that tells you how acid (less than pH 7), neutral (pH 7) or alkaline (pH greater than 7) a soil is. The pH is important as it determines which nutrients are available to the plant. Some nutrients become locked up in acidic soils, while others are unavailable if the soil is too alkaline. To get an accurate picture of your soil pH, take a number of samples from around your garden. A range of pH test kits are available at nurseries and hardware stores.

1 Dig up a small amount of soil with a trowel and break it up until it is fine and crumbly. Place about a tablespoon of soil on the white card supplied with the pH test kit.

2 Squirt a few drops of the colour indicator dye from the kit on the soil and mix it in with the supplied spatula.

3 Dust the top of the soil with powdered barium sulphate. The powder rapidly changes colour.

4 After a few minutes, the colour of the powder will have fully developed. Compare it to the colours on the side of the chart supplied to determine the pH of the soil.

Types of fertiliser

Fertilisers come in lots of different forms, from the manure from your own poultry or stock to products you buy from a garden centre or landscape supplier. Here's a guide to different formulations of manufactured fertilisers which you may want to use to feed your plants.

Milled manure

This is aged manure that has been treated prior to bagging to provide a product with a uniform texture. Milled manures can be safely applied directly to garden beds, soils or potted plants.

Pelletised fertiliser

Manure that's been processed into small pieces to make it easy to bag, handle and disperse. Pelletised materials are often processed to remove the manure smell. The fertiliser breaks down under the action of water and temperature. Pelletised manures can be safely applied to plants and gardens.

Controlled-release fertiliser

This is a small processed ball called a 'prill', containing fertiliser with a cellulose or polymer covering. The surface of the prill is engineered to break down over time, or under certain temperatures, to release its contents. Slow-release fertilisers restrict waste as the materials are released slowly in tune with a plant's needs.

Liquid fertiliser

Any fertiliser that's powdered so it dissolves in water, or a concentrated liquid that's further diluted with water before being applied to the garden, is described as a liquid fertiliser. Mixed in a watering can, liquid fertilisers are the ideal way to apply fertiliser to seedlings, new plants, containerised plants or any plant that needs an energy boost. Liquid fertilisers are also useful where foliar feeding is needed—for example, when soils are highly saline, where there is low root temperature, when the soil pH is higher or lower than the optimum pH for the plant or when roots are compromised or in competition with other plants.

Commercial organic liquid fertilisers are available or you can make your own (see 'Liquid plant foods', opposite).

Hose-on fertiliser

This is a concentrated fertiliser that is applied via a hose. The container of

Milled cow manure

Controlled-release fertiliser

Hose-on fertiliser

Pelletised chicken manure

Soluble fertiliser

RIGHT Drain liquid from the tap at the base of the worm farm as a nutritious liquid feed for the garden. Use water to dilute the nutrient liquid, usually called 'worm wee', before applying it.

FAR RIGHT Once you've drained the liquid from the worm farm it needs to be diluted with water. The ratio is usually 1:10 (wee to water) but aim for the colour of weak black tea.

fertiliser is attached to the nozzle end of the hose. When the tap is turned on, the fertiliser mixes with water from the hose to allow you to apply diluted fertiliser as you water. This is an ideal way to apply fertilisers to large areas such as lawns, or to liquid-feed plants.

Liquid plant foods

It is easy to make your own organic liquid plant food from manure, compost or even green weeds. Liquid decanted from worm farms can also be diluted and applied to plants.

Homemade liquid compost is often referred to as a 'tea', but it is a drink for your plants, not for you!

Manure or compost tea

Fill an old pillowcase or sack with aged animal manure (sheep, goat, chicken, horse, cow) or well-rotted compost and bind the opening with string. Place the sack into a large container such as a plastic rubbish bin or metal drum. Fill the container with water so the bag of manure is submerged. Allow it to steep for several hours. Scoop out the manure-infused liquid. Dilute to the

Tip Re-use the manure-filled bag to make more tea or recycle its contents as mulch.

colour of weak black tea and water it over plants and soil.

Instant vegie tea

You need vegetable scraps and a household blender for this concoction. Mix the vegie scraps in the blender. Pour into a bucket and purée more scraps. Cover the vegie purée with water (about 5 litres to every 1 litre of purée) and allow to steep overnight. Before use, strain the mixture through a sieve. Use the liquid as a tonic for

the garden and put the solids into your worm farm or compost heap.

Worm wee tea

To access the nutrient-rich liquid in your worm farm, open the tap at the base and drain the liquid into a watering can or bucket. Add water until the wee is the colour of weak black tea, then apply it to your vegetables as a liquid plant food.

Tip To avoid particles in these homemade remedies clogging the rose on the watering can, simply leave it off.

Seaweed

Seaweed has long been collected by coastal gardeners to add to their soils as mulch or to be incorporated in compost (see note to the right on gathering seaweed). Salt from seaweed does not have an adverse effect on soil, which means that seaweed gathered from the shore does not need to be washed before it is added to your soil or applied as mulch.

Seaweed has recently become popular as a liquid plant tonic. It is often recommended to treat plants stressed by drought, disease or root damage, to assist when plants are being propagated or transplanted, to give added frost protection, or to sweeten crops such as strawberries or grapes.

Note It is illegal to collect seaweed from beaches in national parks. There may be restrictions on the collection of seaweed from other beaches, including the amount collected or from which part of the beach it may be collected. So, to be on the safe side, check with your local council, environmental office or the National Parks and Wildlife department before collecting seaweed from any beach.

Liquid seaweed is also used to aid the recovery of plants affected by pests or diseases. Once the plant has recovered and begun to show signs of new growth, cut back on seaweed applications and apply a complete fertiliser to feed growth.

Liquid seaweed is made from kelp or sea grasses. It is sold in concentrated liquid form and is diluted before being applied to plants. It contains only very low percentages of nitrogen, phosphorus and potassium (which is why it is classed as a tonic rather than a fertiliser), but it does contain humic acids, which stimulate microbial growth in the soil, which in turn feeds root growth.

Liquid seaweed can be applied year round. When you purchase liquid seaweed to apply to an organic garden, check that the product is made from sustainably harvested seaweeds.

FERTILISER PROBLEMS

Too much fertiliser can be as bad as too little. Here are some problems induced by inappropriate or excessive fertiliser application.

Symptom	Cause	Comment
large, sappy leaves	too much nitrogen	overfed plants can attract aphids which in turn spread virus diseases
burnt leaf tips or edges	fertiliser burn	plants were over-fertilised; fertiliser was applied to dry or drought-stressed plants; fresh manure was applied
death of Australian native plants, proteas	too much phosphorus	many Australian natives and proteas are sensitive to phosphorus; use low-phosphorus formulations
fruit or flower drop	this can be due to over-fertilising	apply fertiliser in small amounts before flowers are initiated
poor flowering	lack of flowers can be due to over-fertilising with nitrogenous fertilisers	change fertiliser; use a formulation to encourage flowering (low nitrogen but higher in phosphorus and potassium)

ABOVE Dilute liquid seaweed before applying it to your garden plants.

Application tips

Fertiliser can be applied in many ways. It can be dug into the soil, applied as a side dressing or simply scattered in and around the plants so that the nutrients are gradually washed into the soil. When the soil is regularly topped with organic mulch, the mulch slowly breaks down to add nutrients to the soil. Fertilisers can also be added to mulches or applied before mulch is added. To avoid damaging plants when adding fertilisers of any kind—whether in the form of compost, manure or manufactured fertiliser—always add them at the recommended rates. To further reduce the risk of harm, apply fertiliser to moist soil—after rain or watering.

RIGHT Spread a controlled-release or pelletised fertiliser before spreading organic mulch. As the mulch breaks down it will also nourish the plants.

Green manure

While most fertilisers are minerals or are derived from aged organic matter, fertiliser can also be added to soil via living plants known as green manure crops. These crops are used to add fertiliser in two ways: directly via their roots, and as they rot down into the soil. See 'Plants to grow for green manure crops', opposite for a list of commonly used plants.

Leguminous plants grown as green manure crops add nitrogen to the soil. This is because legumes have the ability to fix atmospheric nitrogen in the soil via nodules on their roots.

Where plants are being grown in a crop rotation system in the vegetable garden it is wise to incorporate green manure as one of the rotations to help replenish nitrogen without the addition of expensive chemicals. Green manure crops are often grown over winter when the soil is otherwise fallow but they can be grown successfully at any time of the year.

Green manure crops are sometimes referred to as 'cover crops'. They provide a green cover for the soil that stops it being blown away or degraded by heavy rains or harsh sun and they also deter weed growth. Green manure crops can also provide a habitat for beneficial insects, particularly over winter, and feed beneficial soil organisms such as earthworms.

If the crop is being grown to provide stock food or edible seed as well as green manure, allow the plant to flower and the seed to mature before digging the foliage into the soil.

To plant green manure crops buy seed in bulk from local agricultural suppliers or from organic seed suppliers (look for organically certified seed). Legumes are supplied with inoculants to aid nitrogen fixation. Inoculants are suitable for organic systems.

Step-by-Step

HOW TO GROW GREEN MANURE

1 Dig over the soil to ready it for planting and to remove the debris of previous crops. Some seeds need the soil to be moist, so water before sowing. Check the packet.

2 Scatter seeds of any legume, lightly cover then allow it to grow as you would any other vegetable crop.

3 Non-harvestable green manure crops, such as clover, are dug into the soil as the plants begin to flower. This maximises the nutrients that the crop adds to the soil.

PLANTS TO GROW FOR GREEN MANURE CROPS

Green manure crops can be sown after harvesting, when soil is fallow or between rows in an orchard.
Combine several crops to increase benefits. Tall growers can provide support for climbing plants.

Crop	Season (cool/warm)	Comment
alfalfa *Medicago sativa*	cool and warm	adds nitrogen, attracts beneficial insects, tall
broad bean *Vicia faba*	cool	adds nitrogen, tall
buckwheat *Fagopyrum esculentum*	warm	adds potassium, tall
clover, subclover *Trifolium subterraneum*	cool	adds nitrogen, dies down naturally in warm weather so doesn't require cutting; low growing
cowpea *Vigna unguiculata*	warm	adds nitrogen, reduces nematodes, can be harvested as forage for animals, low growing (can climb)
fenugreek *Trigonella foenum-graecum*	cool	adds nitrogen, good choice in cold climates as germinates at low temperatures, low growing
Japanese millet *Echinochloa utilis*	warm	fast growing, tall
linseed *Linum usitatissimum*	warm	provides seed for poultry, low growing
lupins *Lupinus albus*	cool	adds nitrogen, aerates soils, attracts beneficial insects, tall
marigold *Tagetes patula*	warm	deters nematodes, attracts beneficial insects, low growing
millet *Panicum miliaceum*	warm	fast growing, harvest edible seed, tall
mung bean *Vigna radiata*	warm	adds nitrogen, fast growing, low growing
oats *Avena sativa*	cool	helps control nematodes in soil, tall
soy bean *Glycine max*	warm	adds nitrogen, tall
woolly pod vetch *Vicia villosa*	cool	adds nitrogen, attracts predatory insects

CHAPTER 8

Pests and diseases

Why do I need to read this chapter?

Controlling pests and diseases

Huge numbers of pests and diseases can affect fruit and vegetable plants. The knee-jerk method for dealing with such problems is to apply some sort of pesticide, bactericide or fungicide. The decision to grow following organic principles, however, means that, at least in the case of pests, few of the chemical treatments available can be used. Even where organic pesticides are available, the first reaction of an organic gardener should be to think holistically rather than look for an instant fix to the problem.

Stress effect

Pests and diseases often get a foothold when a plant is under stress—short of water, exposed to high temperatures, overcrowded, lacking nutrients, grown out of season or planted in an unsuitable climate. Getting rid of a pest or disease is just part of a larger process that starts with improving the plant's growing conditions. Dispose of affected plant parts with care to avoid spreading the problem to other plants.

Some form of chemical or physical intervention may still be needed, but if the underlying causes of the problem are not addressed, killing the pest or removing the disease may only be a short-term cure.

In an ideal world, of course, plant stress is recognised and corrected before insect pests or diseases occur.

Use the checklist (see 'Plant stress assessment guide', opposite) to examine an ailing plant and its growing situation before deciding what the problem is and how to treat it.

The first part of an overall approach would be to correct any physical problems, such as providing more water to counteract water stress, or providing shade to a plant exposed to too much direct sun. Second, physically remove any pests or cut off disease-affected parts.

Finally, consider treating the pest or disease with an appropriate organic-based remedy, or make your own (see Chapter 12). It is often important to repeat remedies to fully control the pest or disease problem. This should be done at recommended intervals.

PLANT STRESS ASSESSMENT GUIDE

Here's how to examine a plant to work out what stress factors are affecting its health and vigour. Discard factors that aren't having an adverse effect, and concentrate on the problem areas. For suggestions on how to treat environmental problems, see page 114.

1 **Overall plant appearance**

What to look for
A strong, healthy plant with fully turgid leaves, new growth.

Adverse signs
Wilting, dead growth tips, leaf drop.

Physical causes
Water stress, root damage, root disease.

2 **Leaves**

What to look for
Green, shiny undamaged leaves.

Adverse signs
Dull and lifeless leaves, damaged leaves (sunscald, desiccation, insect attack), leaves smaller than normal, torn leaves, such as brown patches (heat damage), fungal spotting, yellow or blotchy leaves, discolouration.

Physical causes
Pests (scale, mealy bug), root damage, hot weather, reflected heat, frost, water damage, hail, plant drying out, soil too wet, wind exposure, lacking fertiliser, too much fertiliser.

3 **Flowers and fruit**

What to look for
Plenty of flowers, fruit a good size and unblemished.

Adverse signs
Fallen buds, discoloured petals, damaged petals, dried flowers, slimy petals, fallen fruit, damaged fruit.

Physical causes
Sun exposure, high temperatures, reflected heat, insect or fungal attack, bird damage, cold weather, frost, wind, drying out (lack of water).

4 **Soil**

What to look for
Soil that's moist but not wet, cool with a good balance of organic matter. Soil should feel crumbly in the hand and water should soak in. Feel the soil. Is it very hot, dry or too wet? If you apply water does it soak in?

Adverse signs
Dry soil, very wet soil, soil that's hard to re-wet when it dries (hydrophobic), hot soil, ants, stones or clods.

Physical causes
Lack of water, sun exposure, lack of organic matter, repeated drying out, high sand content, high clay contact, lack of soil depth.

Tip Root damage can cause many above-soil problems. To find out whether your plant has root damage, hold the stem and move it gently. Is the plant stable in the soil or does it rock as if it is loose? Buffeting by strong winds, storm damage and root death caused by root disease or insect attack can loosen a plant in the soil so it's unable to draw up nutrients and water.

LEFT When diagnosing problems in leaves, look on both sides of the leaf. Here discolouration indicates mosaic virus, which is spread by aphids.

External factors

Many pest and disease problems that affect plants are linked to adverse growing conditions caused by what's happening in the local environment. These include temperatures that are too hot or too cold, weather that's too wet, too humid, too dry or too windy. Climatic conditions overall can be unsuitable (for example cold-loving plants growing in subtropical climates). Soils may also be unsuitable. These external effects can be readily identified by considering factors in the 'Plant stress assessment guide' on page 113.

Correct identification of the problem is important in order to know how it should be treated. One of the first things to work out is whether you are dealing with an insect pest or a disease or whether there is a physical cause for the problem.

Troubleshooting

If you identify that your plant's problem is due to factors in the environment you need to be able to deal with those factors so that the plant can resume normal, healthy growth. Often, quickly remedying adverse growing conditions can stop the plant being attacked by an insect pest or a plant disease. Here are some quick ways to bring your plant back

from the edge by combating adverse environmental conditions.

Lack of water A plant can lack water because it hasn't received enough to compensate for water lost due to weather conditions or because it can't take sufficient water up through its roots. Sometimes soil or potting mix can dry out to a point where it can no longer be easily rehydrated. If a plant is showing signs that it is lacking water the first step is to give it water and to check the water is soaking into the root ball (feel beneath the soil surface). Add an organic soil wetting agent to the water if necessary. If the plant is going to continue to be dried out—either in extreme sun or due to wind—then

shelter it to reduce water loss. This could be with a temporary screen or cover. If the plant has outgrown its position, especially if it is in a pot, repotting or transplanting may be needed. Renewing mulch or adding organic matter to soils can also allow plants to retain more moisture and be less prone to drying out.

Sun exposure Where foliage is showing signs of sunburn, leaves are damaged or plants are wilting repeatedly, then it may be necessary to shade them from the full heat of the sun. Protect plants from too much exposure with a temporary shade screen or cover them with a layer of shadecloth. Long-term protection

RIGHT This damage is caused by an insect—citrus leaf miner—feeding in the leaf tissue.

requires planting taller plants to cast shadow or moving the affected plant to a more sheltered position.

Insect pests

Insects come in all shapes and sizes, from large grasshoppers to mites that are too tiny to be seen with the naked eye. Many insect pests hide by day, feeding only at night so they are rarely seen, while others are hidden in curled leaves, among the roots or concealed under bark or leaves.

Some pests are only damaging at certain stages of their life cycles. Caterpillars, for example, eat plants but their adult forms, moths and butterflies,

do no harm to most plants. Indeed, they can even be helpful in pollination. Here are tips on how to check whether your plant is being attacked by an insect pest.

First up, look for the pest. To do this, examine all parts of the plant. Search under and on top of the leaves, along stems and in the bark. Carefully examine new growth and inside flowers and fruit. Check the plant by day and by night. If you can't find the pest itself look for evidence that it is around. Check for chewed leaves or flowers, holes, lines in the leaves, droppings or webbing. If the pest is not found on the plant it may be visiting it. To see if this is occurring, exclude access to the plant, such as by covering

it with netting, to observe whether the damage stops.

It is also possible to monitor for the presence of insect pests by using traps or lures. Check these regularly. (See page 120 for suggestions on different traps and lures.)

Disease problems

Plant diseases can be mistaken for an insect pest problem or nutrient deficiency. Diseases can attack many different parts of a plant—roots, stems, leaves, buds, flowers and fruit. They may cause a plant to wilt, have discoloured leaves or petals, have holes in leaves or petals, or cause damaged areas on the stem or fruit. Some plant diseases produce obvious symptoms while others do not.

Plant diseases include bacterial, fungal and viral diseases. Some plant diseases are opportunistic secondary infections that invade where physical harm has already occurred—for example, from heat, cold, hail or water damage, or pest damage. Some diseases can be treated, others cannot.

Here are tips to help you work out if your plant has a disease. Look for the disease. Examine all parts of the plant (leaves, stems and tips, flowers and fruit). If the plant is dead, pull it out of the soil and examine the root system.

LEFT Powdery mildew is a disease that affects leaves, shoots and flowers on many plants.

TOP Control cushion scale by applying a horticultural oil spray.

CENTRE Both adults and larvae of the leaf-eating ladybird attack leaves. Pick off by hand when you see them.

BOTTOM Codling moth attacks apples, as well as pears, quince and sometimes walnuts and stone fruit.

Search for indications that disease is present. These may include regular- or irregular-shaped spots or holes, rusty or white pustules, white powder, decay.

Compare this plant to others of the same variety growing nearby. Does it look different?

Treatment methods

Once you have decided whether you are dealing with an insect pest problem or a disease you can begin to work out the exact problem. Pests and diseases can be identified by their appearance or the damage or symptoms they cause.

Some pests and diseases attack a wide range of hosts, others are specific to individual groups of plants. For a list of commonly encountered backyard pests and diseases, see Chapter 11.

As a broad guide, however, insect pests are controlled by physical means (such as squashing or trapping) or an insecticide, while diseases are usually controlled with some type of fungicide or bactericide. Identifying the particular problem allows the correct control method to be used. These can take the form of sprays, soil drenches or baits.

Not all control methods involve chemicals. Control may be achieved through the introduction of insects that prey on a particular pest or disease, a number of which may be obtained commercially (see 'Suppliers of organic products including seeds'

in Chapter 13, page 191). These types of insects are usually called beneficial insects (often shortened to 'beneficials') or biocontrols. Such beneficials include nematodes to control weevil larvae, persimilis bugs to attack two-spotted mite, and particular species of ladybirds to combat aphids or mildew.

Prevention

Where plants are regularly attacked by insect pests or diseases, even when the plants are in good health, it is important to use prevention methods to slow down the rate of attack or perhaps stop it from occurring altogether.

These methods can range from clearing away habitats where insect pests and diseases may survive, to thoroughly cleaning all tools and isolating new plants from the rest of the garden.

Using some or all of the following techniques reduces the incidence of pests and diseases in gardens whether you are growing productive crops or ornamental ones.

Encourage beneficials

It is possible to introduce specific beneficials to the garden that favour certain insect pests, however, there are generally a large number of naturally occurring predatory insects, along with animals such as insectivorous birds, that eat insects or attack them during their life cycle.

RIGHT Practise companion planting. Marigolds can help to control nematodes in the soil and, planted alongside tomatoes, may deter whitefly.

The easiest way to attract a wide range of beneficial insects is to furnish them with both food and shelter such as plants, or an environment that has safe nesting sites and offers protection. This is done by growing plants that provide food for birds in the form of pollen, nectar and seed, and water sources, such as ponds and birdbaths.

Minimising the use of chemicals allows beneficial insects to flourish. Even organically friendly insecticides can be harmful to predators as well as pests, so use with care.

Clean and hygienic

It is also important to clean up sites that provide shelter for unwanted pests and diseases. This can mean removing weeds, such as Cape weed, that provide a food source for pests—particularly over winter—and destroying things in which pests spend part of their life cycle, such as old fruit or plant stakes. It is also important to keep tools that are used in the garden clean, and to sterilise blades on cutting tools such as pruning knives and secateurs that may transfer disease from one plant to another.

A vital way to keep unwanted pests and diseases, and even weeds, away from your garden is not to invite them along in the first place.

This means practising good hygiene. Don't bring in plants that are diseased or show signs of pest damage and isolate new plants brought into your garden to ensure they are not harbouring pests. Also change your clothes and your shoes if you have been into another garden where there may be pest or disease problems. Carefully wash down the wheels of cars or mowers to avoid transferring hitchhiking pests, diseases or weeds.

Crop rotation

Growing annual crops (both vegetables and ornamentals) in different areas from season to season can also help reduce pest and disease populations, particularly in the soil. Crop rotation is discussed in detail in Chapter 6 where there is also a plan for using a crop rotation system in a vegetable garden.

Mingling crops

Growing many different plants together in one space can reduce the presence of insect pests (and some diseases) by confusing the pests. Some insects recognise suitable host plants by their shape and size, while others react to scent. Intermingling plants which are highly aromatic and which have different growth shapes to a plant that's often subject to attack can reduce the problem.

LEFT Mulch inhibits weeds, adds nutrients, regulates soil temperature and retains moisture for healthy plant growth.

Using compost and mulch

Composted organic material and mulch contain beneficial organisms which can combat pests, particularly those in the soil or in the root system of a plant. As the mulch and compost break down the nutrients they contain also provide nourishment, which fuels plant growth and feeds microorganisms in the soil.

Applications of well-rotted compost or aged manure as a mulch layer 2–4 cm thick around plants improves the growth area around the plant's roots and also protects the soil from extreme fluctuations in temperature.

Mulch also prevents weed growth while providing a habitat that may nurture beneficial insects.

Physical barriers

Simple barriers can prevent pests gaining access to certain plants. Cut-off milk cartons or bottles, plastic drink bottles or recycled plastic or polystyrene cups prevent snails, slugs or cutworms reaching seedlings.

Nets and bags can be used to protect larger plants especially while they are fruiting. Place a net over a crop or fit exclusion bags over individual fruits or fruit clusters. Closer to the ground lightweight polypropylene fabric barriers can be used to protect low-growing seedlings.

Barriers (such as a copper collar or sticky band) can be used to encircle a plant's trunk to stop crawling insects gaining access from the ground. Collars around apple trees can prevent codling moth larvae (caterpillars) from reaching fruit as they migrate up the tree from the soil. Sticky bands also stop ants from heading up tree trunks.

LEFT Use a temporary barrier to protect seedlings from snails. Cut-off milk cartons or soft drink bottles do a great job.

Insect traps

Animals and insects can be trapped when lured by the offer of food (for example, cheese or peanut butter in a mouse trap to catch rodents; beer in a saucer to lure snails) or they can be attracted into a trap or a bait station by a scent known as a pheromone. In some cases pheromones are used to lure insects into a trap; in other cases they are not contained but die elsewhere. This is the case with splash baits and lures used in fruit fly control, where the insects are lured to an area where they feed on a bait containing a mixture of protein and insecticide.

Pheromones are natural attractants. Pheromones are the scents that attract insects and animals to one another, particularly for mating. In pest control artificial pheromones are used to attract insects to a trap and away from fruit or flowers, thus reducing adult numbers and also reducing reproduction. Pheromone traps, for example, are used to attract male fruit flies and adult codling moths (traps are available for both male and female moths).

As well as artificial pheromones, mixtures based on carbohydrates or yeast can be used to lure insect pests. Some pheromone traps also contain an insecticide, such as malathion (not considered to be organically compatible) or spinosad (considered acceptable in an organic garden), or a sticky pad. Organic growers should carefully check products to see what type of insecticide they contain. Spinosad is considered safe to use in an organic home garden as if it is a biological insecticide.

Just because a trap is organically compatible doesn't mean it doesn't need to be used with care as you may trap non-target insects or even small animals. Yellow sticky boards, for example, can attract beneficial insects and even small birds so hang them in areas where they are unlikely to do this and always check traps regularly.

Fly traps: fruit flies

Fruit fly traps baited with pheromones are available commercially. Traps are used to indicate the presence of fruit fly and to reduce fly numbers. They must be used in conjunction with other control methods such as splash baits (see page 168) or fruit covers, and good hygiene.

To make your own trap, use a PET bottle and bait made from a yeast-based product. There are many variations on the homemade fruit fly trap so experiment to find out what works.
- PET bottle
- hole-punch
- bait material (e.g. Vegemite or brewer's yeast)
- insecticide (pyrethrum or spinosad)
- water or orange juice
- string or flexible tie-wire

Punch holes in the sides of the bottle, about halfway up, to allow flies to enter the trap. Make two holes in the top of the bottle to thread the string or wire

ABOVE Hang a fruit fly trap near developing fruit to reveal fruit flies and reduce numbers.

to hang the trap. Mix the bait material by combining yeast or Vegemite, a few drops of insecticide, and water or orange juice. Pour mixture into the bottle to just below the entry holes. Thread wire or string through the holes at the top of the bottle and hang the trap in a fruit tree. Several traps are needed per tree.

Fly traps: blowflies and houseflies

There are many commercially available fly traps. Hang them in outdoor areas, around the garden and near animal pens and enclosures to reduce fly numbers. Some fly traps are also placed at ground level. The bait needs to be renewed regularly (usually every couple of weeks while flies are active). To make your own, follow the

ABOVE Yellow or white containers filled with water can attract and collect beetles and bugs.

instructions for a fruit fly trap but use scrap meat and water rather than Vegemite and orange juice.

Sticky barriers

You can buy yellow sticky traps commercially to monitor or reduce the numbers of small flying pests such as white fly or thrips.

To make your own, paint a rectangular board 20–30 cm long and 10–15 cm wide bright yellow. Once the paint has dried, drill a hole in one end and smear the board with Vaseline or some other sticky substance. Using string or tie-wire, hang the board above insect-affected plants or in a greenhouse.

Vaseline can also be used to make a sticky barrier around the trunks of trees to keep ants and some types of caterpillars such as processionary caterpillars or codling moth larvae from travelling up a trunk.

Beer trap for snails

Fill an old saucer with beer and place it in among plants where snails or slugs are active. You can also use a jar part-filled with beer, either placed on its side or sunk into the ground so its top is at ground level.

Collars and barriers

Small insects Cut the bottom off a plastic cup or the top and bottom off a small PET bottle and sink it in the ground around a seedling so the base is at least 5 cm into the soil. This protects the seedling from cutworms, earwigs and slaters. A band of Vaseline smeared around the outside of the trap about halfway up stops climbing insects from scaling the side of the trap.

Possums and rats Wrap smooth, firm plastic sheeting around the trunks of free-standing trees to stop possums climbing into them to attack new shoots, buds or fruit. Position the collar high enough up the trunk that the animal can't leap beyond it.

Bandicoots and brush turkeys Lay wire or plastic mesh over the ground to stop animals that scratch soil or dig for underground insects from rooting up your plants or removing mulch. Secure the wire or mesh firmly to the ground. Providing an alternative food source such as a mulch heap may also reduce foraging.

Know your pest

By understanding the life cycle of a pest insect or plant disease, it is possible to use low-impact chemicals to reduce their numbers and their effect. In winter many pests and diseases are in a resting stage.

Insect pests may be resting as eggs or pupae in soil, leaf litter or under bark on a tree trunk, while fungal diseases may be resting as spore in, on or around a plant. Organically approved chemicals such as lime sulphur, copper sprays and Bordeaux mixture, which may harm plants when they are in leaf or in active growth, can be used to kill the eggs and pupae of pests, or kill resting spores, while plants are dormant and leafless in winter.

By thoroughly spraying the plant and the surrounding ground, populations of problem insects and diseases can be dramatically reduced. Winter washes or winter spray programs work well in conjunction with a winter clean-up (see page 117) and after-winter pruning programs.

Pruning

Removing dead, decaying, diseased or pest-affected parts of a plant can be a quick and efficient way to both remove a pest or disease and to interrupt its life cycle to reduce further attacks. Carried to its extreme, pruning can mean removing an entire plant that is repeatedly attacked.

CHAPTER 9

Maintenance of organic gardens

Why do I need to read this chapter?

Maintaining your garden

Regular care and maintenance is vital in a garden managed on organic principles. Spending a little part of each day in the garden allows you to keep on top of problems and often means that serious issues will be avoided.

Basic daily maintenance involves watering, weeding and tending your plants. If these tasks are done regularly, fewer pests and diseases will strike so the garden is easier to maintain following organic principles. You benefit from this daily attention by harvesting bigger, better crops. This is because your plants are less likely to come under stress when they don't want for water or nutrients and the crops are harvested regularly.

Vegetables are not plants to plant and forget. They require regular attention for good growth and productivity. Daily tasks can include watering, feeding, checking for pest and disease problems, training and weeding. Finally, productive plants require regular harvesting to keep them producing.

Watering

Adequate water is vital for healthy plants, particularly for productive ones such as fruit and vegetable plants. Determining how you can supply water is a first step in planning your organic vegetable garden or orchard.

Vegetables require more water more regularly than fruiting plants. The ideal situation is to have a specific supply of water for the vegetable garden. As water restrictions affect many areas, especially during summer, keen vegetable gardeners who rely on town water supplies need a back-up source of supply such as water tanks, salt-free or low-salt bore water or clean recycled water. In some situations grey water can be used.

The use of mulches and temporary shade can reduce the total quantity of water needed in a vegetable garden, especially in summer, but won't do away with the need for additional water completely.

How do plants use water?

Plants take up water from the soil and exude it through tiny holes in their leaves called stomates. The process of losing water from leaves is called transpiration. It helps keep plants cool and also allows them to continuously draw nutrients through their cells from the roots in the soil.

Plants that have adapted to growing in hot climates may have systems that allow them to cut their rates of transpiration by drooping their leaves, closing stomates during the heat of the day, or making the leaf surface less exposed to the sun by coverings of fine hairs, reflective colouration (often silvery) or some other method.

What sort of water?

Rainwater from water tanks This is probably the best source of water for vegetable gardens. To get strong water pressure, install a pump or elevate the tank on a stand.

Bore water Test bore water to measure the levels of dissolved salts it contains. This test is done with a conductivity meter and gives an EC reading (electrical conductivity). Also use a pH meter to test the pH (that is, level of dissolved ions) of bore water before it is used for irrigation.

Clean recycled water This covers water collected, usually in a bucket, that would otherwise run to waste, such as the water used for rinsing vegetables or which runs from the shower before the hot water arrives. This type of water is particularly handy for use on herbs and vegies growing in containers.

Grey water In many areas it is illegal to use untreated grey water (water derived from showers and laundry) on edible crops. In particular, it is unadvisable to use it on leafy crops. Grey water can contain bacteria that could be a health risk when it contacts the leaves of edibles such as silverbeet, spinach, lettuce—the part of the plant that is harvested for eating. Before using grey water, check your local authority's regulations and restrictions and consider installing a treatment system (see 'Grey water treatment options' on page 126). The other concern with the use of grey water is that it may contain high levels of salts from laundry detergents. Over time grey water can affect soil pH and soil quality. It should not be applied continuously to one area and should not be applied when the soil is already wet. The addition of gypsum can help rectify soil that has been damaged by over-application of grey water that's high in salts.

LEFT While watering inspect crops for signs of pests and remove weeds.

RIGHT Having rainwater from tanks helps to beat local water restrictions but don't waste it. A timer helps control use.

FAR RIGHT Rainwater tanks collect water from the house roof as well as from sheds and out buildings providing a reliable source for gardens.

Grey water treatment options

Untreated grey water cannot be stored for more than 24 hours and should not be applied to the edible parts of crops.

If only grey water is available to maintain a vegetable garden or fruit trees, you will have to install some form of grey water treatment system. The system you choose should provide more than filtration—it should also remove bacteria and contaminants from the water.

As well as rotating grey water use to different parts of the garden on a daily/weekly basis, check that any powders or liquids used in the washing machine are not adding an unacceptable level of salts such as boron and phosphorus. Use only laundry products that are compatible with grey water recycling. Avoid using additives such as fabric softeners.

Where grey water is used, it should be applied to the soil surface by drippers or a soaker hose. Do not apply over foliage via a sprinkler or with a hose nozzle.

Watering frequency

One of the most often asked plant care questions is how frequently should plants be watered. Plants should be watered when they are dry but before they become water stressed—indicated by wilting, leaf loss and contraction of soil.

Frequency of watering depends on the plant, its growing conditions and the weather. Plants need more water when the weather is hot and/or windy, they are growing in sandy soil or they are producing new growth, flowers or fruit. Large plants in small pots need more water than similar plants in the ground.

The key to applying the optimum amount of water is to read the plant (that is look for signs of wilting) and to feel the soil to see how moist or dry it is. Check the soil around the root zone, not just on the surface.

Allowing plants, particularly productive plants, to dry out can have serious consequences. They may abort their flowers or fruit, change their growth cycle from leafy growth to flowering and seeding (termed bolting) or even die prematurely.

Over-watering can be detrimental as well. Waterlogged conditions can lead to root rot or root death. Plants can suffer dieback and/or drop fruit and flowers. Leafy vegetables may be attacked by fungal problems.

Getting watering right improves the health and vigour of plants and reduces the need for control measures against pests and diseases.

Timing of watering

Debate rages about just when is the best time to water plants, with early morning or evening usually recommended. Good timing is about reducing water loss through evaporation from soils, as well as providing the best results for the plant.

There is no hard and fast rule about when to water—although where you are subjected to water restrictions, timing may be controlled by your water authority.

The bottom line, however, is that plants should be provided with water when they need it and when you can supply it. Often, watering to maintain strong, healthy plant growth is needed

RIGHT Attach water timers on all external taps to reduce over-watering. Timers automatically shut down the water supply reducing waste.

in both the morning and the evening, especially where little rain has fallen and the weather is hot and windy.

If automated timer-controlled watering systems are used, watering during the night when the air is cool and still may be best. At this time, water pressure is often at its peak and evaporation rates are low.

Watering in the early morning provides water for the plants to draw on throughout the day and can reduce the effects of heat. Water lying on the leaves will evaporate, reducing the likelihood of fungal diseases taking hold. When a hot day is forecast it is prudent to be out watering early.

Plants that wilt or become water stressed during the day should be watered when this occurs. There is a widely held belief that watering in the heat of the day can cause harm—on the other hand, if plants become badly water stressed, they can die unless they are watered and, if possible, shaded. Watering is unlikely to do any harm, and studies have shown that wet foliage doesn't necessarily lead to plant death or even leaf burn.

How to apply water

Watering a plant may seem like the easiest task in the world. You point a hose or a sprinkler at it, splash on some water for a while and you're done. Wrong. Getting watering right is about getting the necessary amount of water to the base of the plant where it soaks into the root system.

RIGHT Install a rain gauge to record rainfall and also to assess how much water may have been added to your water storage tanks.

If you are dependent on water from a rainwater tank, invest in a small pump to ensure strong and even water pressure from whichever water delivery system you are using—hose, sprinkler or drip irrigation.

An irrigation system is the most efficient way of getting water to plants. Plus, if you install an automatic timer, all you need to do is set the number of days per week you want it to water and the length of time and it'll turn itself on as programmed. Before you start, draw a rough plan of your garden and map out the path of the irrigation system. From this, you can work out the amount of pipe you need and the number and type of fittings.

Restrictions regarding the use of spray heads vary around Australia, so check with your local water board before designing your system. Also check whether local authorities require you to have a backflow valve installed by a plumber to stop irrigation water, particularly from rainwater tanks, flowing back into the mains water system. Your irrigation supplier can help with all these questions.

Carry out a maintenance check every couple of months looking for leaks and blockages, and adjust the timer according to the season and the water needs of the plants.

Step-by-Step

HOW TO LAY AN IRRIGATION SYSTEM

Essential tools *Pliers, knife or cutting tool to cut pipe, hole-punch, tool box to hold small fittings.*

Irrigation fittings *Timer, 19 mm polypipe, 13 mm polytube, 4 mm polypipe, micro-spray heads, adjustable drippers, clamps, 13 mm and 19 mm joiners, both in a range of shapes, 4 mm joiners, end stops, goof plugs (to fix mistakes), wire pegs.*

1 Install the timer. Some timers have a simple dial that you turn every time you want to water. Simple automatic timers are battery operated; more complex units allow the programming of multiple irrigation lines and must be connected to mains power.

2 Use 19 mm pipe from the tap and around the outer edges of the system. Lay it out on the ground where it is to go.

3 Attach the pipes together with joiners. Secure the pipe to the joiners with a clamp, and tighten with pliers.

4 Use 13 mm polytube to run through the garden. Set it out in rows about 30 cm apart. Attach it to the 19 mm pipe at either end with a joiner and secure with clamps.

5 Make holes in the pipe with the hole-punch where the drippers and spray heads are to be positioned.

6 If you make a hole in the wrong place, push in a goof plug to seal the hole.

7 Attach a 4 mm joiner to the end of the dripper or spray head pipe, if needed, then insert into the pipe.

8 Position the drippers and spray heads. Drippers are good to use on individual plants as they deliver water only to a small area. Spray heads cover a larger area and are best used in the middle of a group of plants, or for watering new seedlings.

9 Turn on the tap to flush out any dirt or debris that's got into the pipes during installation. Once the water is running clear, insert an end stop into the end of every pipe and secure with a clamp.

10 Hold the pipes in place on the ground with wire pegs. If you want to conceal a pipe, cover it with mulch.

Tip To make it easier to push pipes onto the fittings, hold the pipe in hot water for 20–30 seconds, or until softened.

How to use a hose

Most water restrictions force gardeners to use hoses as the main method for delivering water to plants. Where there's no form of irrigation installed, hoses are also the most convenient method of watering.

In most instances, however, watering by hose means under-watering. Gardeners simply underestimate how much time is needed for sufficient water to soak into the soil to water the roots.

Here's how to make sure you get watering right if you are watering with a hose. If you are outside watering in hot sun, make sure you are adequately protected from sunburn with hat, sunglasses, long sleeves and sunscreen.

Watering rules

Hose diameter Large diameter hoses deliver more water and narrower hoses deliver less water. If you have a large area to water and good water pressure, use a large diameter hose.

Best nozzle type Most water restrictions require that hose nozzles are trigger-operated so they can be turned off to avoid wasting water.

RIGHT Measure fertilisers carefully and dilute at the recommended rate. Add the fertiliser to water then stir or swirl watering can to dissolve.

Long-armed nozzles, also called water breakers, make watering easier by allowing you to reach further.

Systematic approach Divide the garden into sections based on watering needs, with some areas such as pots or vegetables requiring daily watering and others needing water at less frequent intervals. Water the daily watering zones each day and rotate watering the other parts of the garden so each area receives the amount of water it needs regularly.

Water the roots Direct the water to the base of each plant, allowing the water to soak into the soil and reach the root system. If the water begins to pond, move on to the next plant while the water soaks in. Then go back and water again.

Feel the soil To make sure the water is reaching its target—the roots—feel below the soil surface with your fingers. The soil should be moist to a depth of several centimetres.

Watering and feeding

Fertilisers can be dissolved in water to allow feeding and watering at the same time. Liquid plant foods are just one of the options open to gardeners needing

to provide extra nutrients. Liquid feeding gives plants an extra boost and the effects can be rapid. Liquid fertilisers are also less likely than granular or fresh animal manure products to burn the plant or to provide too much in the way of nutrients.

Actively growing vegetables benefit from fortnightly applications of liquid plant food. As with any fertiliser, always apply following the dose recommendation on the container to avoid damaging the plants.

While instant access to nutrients is a benefit supplied by liquid plant foods, there are some drawbacks. If the soil or potting mix is not water receptive, the nutrients can be quickly lost as the water flows away from rather than into the plant's root system.

LEFT Metal fittings are more expensive than plastic but more durable and longer lasting.

RIGHT When using micro-irrigation sprayers or sprinklers check that the water is reaching the soil..

Kicking the weeds

The usual method for dealing with weeds is to kill them with herbicides (also called weedicides). Herbicides are chemicals that kill weeds. Some affect specific types of weeds, such as broad-leafed weeds, while others kill any green plant.

The concerns about herbicides are their immediate effect on the soil and surrounding plants and their longer-term effect on other organisms if they move into waterways or on other plants if they enter the soil.

The most widely used herbicide in domestic situations is glyphosate. Although this herbicide has little residual action as it is broken down

quickly in the soil, its use can cause problems in waterways. If you are using glyphosate for weed control, observe the cautions for its use. If applying it near a waterway, use a formulation that's safe to use near water.

There are a few herbicides based on relatively benign household chemicals such as salt and vinegar. Some are available commercially, but recipes for homemade versions are given in Chapter 12, page 182. Other organically friendly herbicides are based on plant extracts such as pine oil.

Weeding without herbicides

In most cases an organic vegetable gardener avoids using herbicides to remove grass and weeds. This leaves you with some form of physical removal to keep on top of weeds.

In general, hoeing is the most effective way of removing weeds. Using a hoe you can lightly tend the soil between rows of vegetables, cutting off weeds below the soil surface but not damaging the roots of your crops.

Larger weeds can be removed using a hoe with three prongs or tines. The tines are used to get down into the soil and lift the plant by its roots. As well as being effective tools to remove weeds, hoes are also operated from a standing position. Not having to bend over is better for your back.

When you are weeding between small plants and seedlings, however, you will have to get 'down and dirty' and resort to weeding by hand with a fork.

Lots of weeds

Where there are lots of weeds or unwanted plants to deal with—for example, establishing a vegetable patch or orchard—the scale of work required can seem daunting.

Removing large areas of weed or grass without using herbicides may involve digging, raking, rotary hoeing, using a whipper snipper (also called a strimmer), or using a machine such as a turf cutter to remove the grass and top layer of soil. This is less physically demanding than simply digging and means that the turf can be relaid elsewhere in the garden.

Grass and weeds can also be killed by using a covering to exclude light—cardboard, old carpet or plastic film (see 'Soil solarisation', opposite).

The cover needs to be left long enough to kill the grass and its roots before the area is dug over and roots and runners are removed.

Where the covers are biodegradable, the vegetable patch can be built up on top of them following no-dig gardening principles as outlined in Chapter 3, page 39.

Other sources of heat can also be used to kill weeds. These can include hot water, steam, and mini-flame weeders in small areas, and larger flame weeders for bigger areas.

Soil solarisation

The viability of weed seeds present in soil can be reduced by a process called soil solarisation. Cheap, environmentally friendly and safe, soil solarisation is literally harnessing the heat of the sun to kill seeds before they germinate.

If the garden area has been weedy in the past, chances are there are lots of seeds dormant in the soil. These will continue to germinate as the soil is cultivated, watered and fertilised, creating a huge maintenance problem in the vegetable patch.

First remove existing grass and weeds and dig over the soil. Then cover the area with a large piece of clear plastic. The heat from the sun shining through the plastic warms the soil, killing seeds and soil-borne pathogens. After about six weeks the soil should be weed free and ready to plant and cultivate.

This process works best during sunny periods in summer. If the weather is cool or cloudy, leave the plastic in place for longer.

LEFT When hand weeding, use a hand tool such as a fork to prise roots from the soil. Squat or kneel rather than bend to prevent a sore back.

Weeding out weeds

One of the things that happens when you dig over soil to remove grass and weeds in preparation for planting is that more weeds appear.

These new weeds germinate in the disturbed soil from seeds lying dormant. Weeds are plants that grow to take advantage of disturbed soil and many germinate if exposed to light.

To get rid of these weeds, lightly hoe over the ground to disturb the seedlings before they get a chance to develop. Repeat the process a few days later—and again, if necessary.

Note When tethering an animal to help clear weeds use a strong collar with a swivel attachment and attach the tether to an anchor point also with a swivel attachment. Move tethers for access to fresh feeding spots.

If at this point you are not ready to plant, cover the cleared area with a layer of organic mulch. This does several things—hinders weed germination, protects the soil surface from wind, heat and heavy rain, and encourages beneficial organisms, including earthworms, to start colonising the soil.

Animal helpers

Animals such as poultry (particularly chickens) and goats can be used in place of herbicides to help clear weedy areas in preparation for making a vegetable garden.

Chickens clear away weeds, old vegetables and unwanted plants by pecking and scratching. They also add manure to the soil. If the garden is fenced and predator proof, the brood can be left loose, or you can manage them in a portable chicken coop (see illustration). Move the coop as each area is cleared. Cover the cleared zone with a layer of mulch until you are ready to plant.

Goats are useful for clearing long grass and brambles such as blackberries, which are difficult to remove by hand. Goats need to be contained by strong fencing or by being tethered as they can climb into trees and damage them, and get into areas where their presence is not required and eat things you want to keep. It is safest to fence animals in rather than to tether them, but tethering can be useful to clean up weeds.

LEFT Smaller, mobile chook pens allow you to move the chickens around. These coops are often referred to as chicken tractors.

ABOVE Regularly remove spent crops. These can be added to the compost heap or fed to chickens.

RIGHT Chickens like these Silkies look decorative in the garden but they can scratch up new plants and cause damage, so keep an eye on them.

10 minutes a day

Even if you are busy, always spend at least 10 minutes a day in your garden. Take a quick walk around to make sure everything is in order.

Use this time to check for any dry plants and water them, pick ripe crops and scout for insects. Have a bucket handy to collect any weeds you notice and pair of secateurs with you to snip off broken, diseased or spent plant material.

CHAPTER 10

A–Z of edible plants

Why do I need to read this chapter?

- To discover the size and productive seasons for a range of edible plants.

- To find out about their growing needs.

- To gather information on propagation, pollination and harvesting.

Here are some of the most commonly grown fruit and vegetable plants. Where growing information is similar to another plant, refer to that plant for 'Growing information'. The list is arranged alphabetically by common name.

A

ALMOND *See* PEACH

APPLE
Malus x *domestica*

Family Rosaceae

Other edible plants grown in the same way Crabapple, medlar, pear, quince.

Plant type Deciduous tree.

Size To 10 m high, 2–3 m wide. Dwarf varieties, or varieties grafted on dwarf rootstock such as 'M27', are available.

Climate & aspect Cool to temperate. Full sun. Apples require a period of winter chill before flowering so grow best in cold regions. In temperate zones select low-chill varieties such as 'Fuji', 'Gala', 'Pink Lady'.

Planting Winter (bare-rooted), year round for potted plants.

Propagation Grafted or budded onto disease-resistant understock. Apples can be grown from seed but varieties do not come true to type and can take many years to begin flowering and fruiting. Some varieties

ABOVE Apples are best suited to mild climates with winter chilling and need a cross-pollinator such as another apple variety or a crabapple to form fruit.

can be grown from hardwood cuttings taken in winter.

Flowering & pollination Late winter to spring. Apples require another apple variety flowering at the same time for cross-pollination for fruit production. Crabapples (*Malus* spp.) may also provide pollen for cross-pollination. Apples are bee-pollinated.

Harvest Late summer to autumn (based on variety). Fruit stores well in cool, dark conditions. Excess fruit can be dried, bottled, frozen, juiced or made into cider.

Growing information Prune in summer (after harvest) or in winter when bare. Apples are pruned to encourage the growth of fruiting spurs. Protect blossom from late frost. For larger fruit, thin the crop in early to mid summer. Hail in summer can damage crops. Provide ample water while fruiting. Remove mummified fruit in late autumn and winter to restrict spread of

disease. Spray trees with copper-based sprays in winter while dormant and at bud burst to control scab.

Pests Aphids, codling moth, fruit fly, thrips, woolly aphids. Apples are also attacked by birds and may require netting. Rats and mice can attack stored fruit.

Diseases Bitterspot, brown rot, canker, fireblight (not present in Australia), powdery mildew, scab (select scab-resistant varieties).

APRICOT
Prunus armeniaca

Family Rosaceae

Other edible plants grown in the same way Almond, peach, plum.

Plant type Deciduous tree.

ABOVE Apricots form attractive trees and are one of the first of the stone fruit to begin cropping. They are ideal in a Mediterranean climate and benefit from a hot summer.

ABOVE Artichokes are harvested before the bud begins to open.

Size 6–8 m high, 4.5 m wide.

Climate & aspect Cold, temperate and Mediterranean climates. Full sun. Apricots need a period of winter chilling with warm summers for ripening.

Planting Winter (bare-rooted), year round for potted plants.

Propagation Budded on to various rootstocks including apricot, plum and peach. Plum rootstock is preferred in heavier soils or more humid summer climates. Can be grown from seed but varieties may not come true.

Flowering & pollination Late winter to early spring (flowers may be frost affected in cold zones). Self-fertile, bee-pollinated.

Harvest Late spring to mid summer (depending on variety). Excess fruit can be made into jam or frozen.

Growing information Winter prune to remove dieback and dead wood. Protect flowers from late frost. Thin crop in late spring or early summer. Prune after cropping in late summer. Spray with copper- or lime-based sprays in winter to control disease.

Pests Aphids, fruit fly, scale.

Diseases Dieback, gummosis, silver leaf.

ARTICHOKE
Cynara scolymus

Family Asteraceae

Other edible plants grown in the same way Cardoon.

Plant type Perennial.

Size 1 m high, 1 m wide.

Climate & aspect All areas, full sun.

Planting Autumn to early spring (suckers), late summer in subtropical to tropical areas (suckers). Seeds are sown in spring.

Propagation Suckers. Divide and replant after 3–4 years when production decreases.

Flowering & pollination Spring, self-fertile.

Harvest Spring. Harvest buds before opening. The peeled stem is also edible.

Growing information Leave clumps undisturbed. Cut back to 30 cm in autumn.

Pests Few.

Diseases Few.

ASIAN GREENS
See LETTUCE

ASPARAGUS
Asparagus officinalis

Family Asparagaceae

Other edible plants grown in the same way Bamboo (harvested for shoots).

Plant type Herbaceous perennial.

Size 1.5 m high, 30 cm wide.

Climate & aspect All areas (best in mild climates). Full sun.

Planting Winter (crowns), spring (seed).

Propagation Grafted or budded. Some varieties can be grown from cutting.

Flowering & pollination Spring. Asparagus grows as separate male and female plants. Females produce red berries (remove plants). Male plants have larger spears than female and are preferred. Male and female plants are needed for seed production but for spears male plants are preferred.

Harvest Spring (for around 10 weeks). Summer-pruned plants may produce an autumn crop. Cut spears below ground at 15–20 cm long before tips open.

Growing information Plants are long lived so prepare ground well with compost and aged manure before planting. Water well while actively growing. Fertilise in spring and summer. Cut back in late autumn or winter. The best shoots, called spears, are produced after the second or third year of growth.

Pests Few.

Diseases Few.

AVOCADO
Persea americana

BELOW Tender asparagus spears are produced in early spring. Plant crowns in winter.

BELOW Avocado is at its most productive in subtropical and tropical climates.

Family Lauraceae

Other edible plants grown in the same way Citrus.

Plant type Evergreen tree.

Size 9 m high, 3 m wide. Dwarf varieties available.

Climate & aspect All but cold zones. Full sun to part shade.

Planting All year for potted plants.

Propagation Named, grafted varieties fruit in 3–5 years. Plants are often seed grown. Seed-grown trees may take up to 7 years to fruit.

Flowering & pollination Spring. Cross-pollination with compatible varieties produces more reliable crops. Varieties are classified as A or B. Wind-pollinated.

Harvest Autumn onwards (depending on variety). Fruit ripens off the tree.

Growing information Plant in very well drained soil. Apply fruiting fertiliser (such as citrus food) during flowering and growing season (spring to summer). Keep well watered in dry weather.

Pests Bats, possums, rats.

Diseases Anthracnose, root rot. Grafted plants are more disease-resistant.

B

BABACO *See* BANANA

BAMBOO *See* ASPARAGUS

BANANA
Musa spp. and named varieties

Family Musaceae

Other edible plants grown in the same way Babaco, pawpaw, plantain.

Plant type Herbaceous perennial.

Size 3–9 m high (depending on variety), 3 m wide.

Climate & aspect Tropical, subtropical, temperate (frost-free areas). Full sun.

Planting Spring (suckers), all year in tropics.

Propagation Grown from suckers. In Australia, bananas are subject to government controls in commercial banana-growing districts to reduce spread of disease. Check with your local Department of Agriculture or Primary Industries about restrictions in your area.

Flowering & pollination Year round in warm climates, spring to summer in cooler zones. Separate male and female flowers but true female flowers are self-fertile. Domesticated fruit does not produce seed.

Harvest Fruit is harvested 12–18 months after planting when top bananas begin to ripen and fruit loses its angular shape. In cooler areas bananas are usually harvested in autumn. Green fruit can be ripened off the plant. Excess fruit can be dried.

Growing information Remove unwanted suckers. Cut down stem after fruit is harvested. To prevent pest attack and encourage ripening, cover hands of fruit with an open-ended bag (known as a blue or bunch bag). Bananas have high fertiliser needs so dig in plenty of organic matter before planting, apply more organic fertiliser and mulch and water regularly, especially in summer.

ABOVE Bananas take many months to form fruit but are well worth the wait.

Pests Aphids, bats, birds, rats.

Diseases Bunchy top, Panama disease. Remove and destroy diseased plants.

BASIL, SWEET BASIL
Ocimum basilicum

Family Lamiaceae

Other edible plants grown in the same way Most annual herbs, including marjoram, mint, oregano, parsley, sage.

Plant type Annual herb.

Size 30–40 cm high, 20 cm wide.

Climate and aspect All areas. Full sun to part shade (especially in hot areas).

Planting Spring to summer (seed or seedlings). Grow year round in subtropical and tropical zones.

ABOVE Basil is a fast-growing annual herb that's easy to start from seed.

Propagation Seed or seedlings.

Flowers & pollination Summer to autumn. Self-fertile; bee-attracting.

Harvest Spring to autumn. Excess leaves can be made into pesto, dried or preserved in oil.

Growing information Encourage bushy, leafy growth by tip pruning. Liquid feed every 2–3 weeks during summer and keep plants well watered. Prolong growth by removing flower buds. Plants die back after flowering or at first frost. Late frost may kill early plantings so delay planting in cold districts or protect seedlings in frost-prone areas.

Pests Aphids, caterpillars, slugs, snails, whitefly.

Diseases Few.

BAY TREE
Laurus nobilis

Family Lauraceae

Other edible plants grown in the same way Lemon myrtle, rosemary.

Plant type Evergreen tree.

Size 7–8 m high, 3 m wide. Can be kept shorter by regular pruning.

Climate & aspect Cold, Mediterranean, temperate. Full sun. Shelter from frost and hot or cold winds while young.

Planting All year.

Propagation Cuttings (semi-hardwood in summer), layering, division, seed.

Flowers & pollination Spring. Self-fertile; bee-attracting.

Harvest Year round.

Growing information Grow in well-drained soil. Prune spring to late summer to shape. Fertilise in spring and after pruning. Can be grown in pots.

Pests Ants, scale.

Diseases Sooty mould.

BEANS
Phaseolus vulgaris

Family Fabaceae

Other edible plants grown in the same way Runner beans (*P. coccineus*) are perennial climbing beans grown as an annual. They do best in cool climates. Snake beans (*Vigna unguiculata* subsp. *sesquipedalis*) do best in subtropical and tropical areas. Lima beans (*P. lunatus*) are grown for their dry seeds. Broad

ABOVE Bay trees can be grown in large containers as a dense evergreen shrub.

beans are grown during cooler seasons (planted in autumn or early spring in cold areas).

Plant type Annual vine (climbing beans); dwarf or bush beans available.

Size 3 m high, 1 m wide. Dwarf varieties under 1 m.

Climate & aspect All areas. Full sun.

Planting Spring to early summer (year round in subtropical and tropical areas).

Propagation Seed, seedlings.

Flowers & pollination Spring to autumn. Self- and insect-pollinated. Flowering and pollination is reduced in extremely hot or dry weather.

Harvest Spring to autumn (year round in subtropical and tropical areas), 8–10 weeks (dwarf beans) or 10–12 weeks (climbing beans) after sowing. High temperatures at flowering may reduce harvest. Pick when tender. Dry or shell beans such as

ABOVE Beans are one of the most productive of vegetable crops. 'Borlotti' is grown for dried seed.

'Borlotti' are left on the vine to harden before harvest.

Growing information Plant after frost in cold areas when soil temperature rises above 10°C. Dig in complete fertiliser before planting. Take care not to put seeds in direct contact with fertiliser at planting. Water well after seeds germinate. Liquid feeding or side dressings boost yield. Apply from flowering. Beans are legumes so they add nitrogen to soils via nodules on their roots. Support climbing beans on a frame, trellis or tripod.

Pests Aphids, bean fly, thrips, whitefly.

Diseases Rust, halo blight.

BEETROOT
Beta vulgaris subsp. *vulgaris*

Family Chenopodiaceae

Other edible plants grown in the same way Most root vegetables (including kohl rabi, swede, turnip), kale (also known as

ABOVE Beetroot is a delicious and nutritious root vegetable. Try baby beets in pots.

ABOVE Blackberries are roadside weeds in many areas. In gardens grow thornless varieties to make harvesting and management easier.

cavolo nero), mustard.

Plant type Biennial (grown as an annual).

Size 30 cm high, 20 cm wide.

Climate & aspect All. Full sun.

Planting Spring to autumn (cold to temperate), late summer to late spring (subtropical and tropical).

Propagation Seed.

Flowers & pollination Plants bolt to flower and seed if stressed or grown out of season. Select slow-bolt varieties to avoid early seeding. This root crop is harvested before flowering.

Harvest 10–12 weeks from sowing seed. Store in refrigerator or bottle excess. Young leaves can be harvested for salads.

Growing information Thin seedlings to 20 cm apart. Liquid feed regularly for fast growth. Beetroot may suffer from boron deficiency that can lead to deformed

growth and hollow roots. Add boron to deficient soils prior to planting.

Pests Few.

Diseases Few.

BLACKBERRY
See BRAMBLES

BOYSENBERRY
See BRAMBLES

BRAMBLES
Rubus spp.

Family Rosaceae

Other edible plants grown in the same way All deciduous berry plants including blackberry, boysenberry, gooseberry, raspberry.

Plant type Bush or vine.

Size 2 m high, 2–6 m wide.

Climate All except tropics.

Planting Winter (bare-rooted).

Propagation Suckers, cuttings.

Flowering & pollination Spring. Self-fertile.

Harvesting Summer to autumn (depending on variety).

Growing information Keep weed free, prune in winter to encourage young vigorous wood and to remove dead canes. Apply fertiliser in spring as new growth appears. Thornless varieties are easiest to maintain and harvest. Can become invasive and may be spread by seed. Blackberries are weedy in many areas.

Pests Fruit fly, birds.

Diseases Rust.

ABOVE Broccoli is grown from seed or seedlings. The heads of unopened flower buds are what are harvested but stems are also edible.

ABOVE Carrots are everyone's favourite and grow best in deep, well-drained soils.

BROAD BEANS *See* BEANS

BROCCOLI
Brassica oleracea

Family Brassicaceae

Other edible plants grown in the same way Brussels sprouts, cabbage, calabrese, cauliflower.

Plant type Annual.

Size 40 cm high, 30 cm wide.

Climate & aspect All (best in cool to temperate climates). Full sun.

Planting Year round in subtropics, autumn to winter in tropics, summer to early autumn in temperate climates, late spring to early autumn in cool climates. Planting too late in the season can lead to poor growth and poor yields. Plants may bolt to seed.

Propagation Seed (sow directly in prepared beds or in seed trays).

Flowering & pollination Harvest before flowers open (broccoli is the bud). Harvesting the top head encourages side shoots to bud. Self-fertile but only allow flowering to occur in order to collect seed.

Harvesting 18–20 weeks.

Growing information Fertilise with liquid feed or side dressings for quick plant growth. Harvest top when buds tightly closed to encourage second crop of side branches.

Pests Aphids, caterpillars.

Diseases Few.

BRUSSELS SPROUTS
See BROCCOLI

C

CABBAGE *See* BROCCOLI

CALABRESE *See* BROCCOLI

CAPSICUM *See* TOMATO

CARDOON *See* ARTICHOKE

CARROT
Daucus carota

Family Apiaceae

Other edible plants grown in the same way Daikon, parsnip, radish.

Plant type Biennial grown as an annual.

ABOVE Ceylon spinach, a leafy climber, is an excellent source of green spinach-like leaves to grow year round in warm climates and through summer in cooler areas.

Size 30 cm high, 10 cm wide.

Climate & aspect All. Full sun.

Planting All year (late winter to summer in cool and temperate climates).

Propagation Seed. Mix seed with sand for more even distribution and to reduce thinning. Sow in situ.

Flowering & pollination Summer to autumn. Harvest before flowering occurs. Self-fertile (only allow to seed if seed collection is desired).

Harvesting 3–4 months from sowing.

Growing information Sow in well-prepared beds with added fertiliser (do not use fresh manure). Ensure soil is free of weeds and stones (poorly prepared soil leads to short or deformed carrots). Germination 10 days to 3 weeks. Keep soil moist and lightly mulched. Thin after germination. Encourage quick growth with liquid feeding every 2–3 weeks.

Pests Few.

Diseases Few.

CAULIFLOWER
See BROCCOLI

CAVOLO NERO
See BEETROOT

CEYLON SPINACH, MALABAR SPINACH
Basella alba

Family Basellaceae

Other edible plants grown in the same way New Zealand spinach, sweet potato (kumara).

Plant type Sprawling vine.

Size 2 m+.

Climate & aspect All (best in warm, frost-free areas, protect from cold in winter). Full sun.

Planting Spring to summer.

Propagation Seed or cuttings.

Flowering & pollination Remove flowers to keep in leafy growth.

Harvesting Harvest young leaves and shoots as soon as plants are growing well, prolific in summer.

Growing information Train up a tripod or along a trellis for ease of harvesting.

Pests Leaf-eating pests.

Diseases Few.

CHERRY *See* PEACH

CHILLI *See* TOMATO

CHINESE GOOSEBERRY
See KIWIFRUIT

CHIVES
Allium schoenoprasum

Family Alliaceae

Other edible plants grown in the same way Garlic chives, shallots, spring onion.

Plant type Perennial herb.

Size 30 cm.

Climate & aspect All. Full sun to shady.

Planting Spring (any time, warm climates).

Propagation Seed (spring) or divide clumps in autumn.

Flowering & pollination Summer to autumn. Self-fertile.

Harvesting Begin picking leaves 90 days after sowing. Leave 5 cm leaf base when harvesting to allow regeneration. Buds and flowers are also edible.

Growing information Forms a strong leafy clump. Water to establish and during extended dry periods. Liquid feed occasionally. Can be grown in pots.

Pests Aphids.

Diseases Few.

CHOKO
Sechium edule

Family Cucurbitaceae

Other edible plants grown in the same way Ceylon spinach, sweet potato.

Plant type Climber.

Size 3 m+.

Climate & aspect All (best in warm, frost-free). Full sun.

Planting Autumn to spring.

Propagation Seed or cuttings.

Flowering & pollination Late summer. Self-fertile.

Harvesting Late summer to autumn.

BELOW Chives are grown for their tasty leaves but the flowers are also edible.

BELOW Traditionally grown over the outdoor 'dunny' or back fence, chokos are a common crop. They are most tender harvested when they are still small.

Growing information Very vigorous. Train up a tripod or along a trellis for ease of harvesting. Water when dry and fertilise in spring to encourage strong growth.

Pests Few.

Diseases Few.

CITRUS
Citrus spp.

Family Rutaceae

Other edible plants grown in the same way Australian native finger limes, coffee, cumquat, grapefruit, lemon, lime, lillypilly, mandarin, mango, orange, pomegranate, tangerine, tea.

Plant type Evergreen tree.

Size 1.8–4.5 m high, 1.8 3 m wide (depending on species and variety). Dwarf varieties available.

Climate & aspect All (best in warm, frost-free areas, protect from winter cold). Full sun.

Planting Spring to summer.

Propagation Grafted plants preferred. Understock is seed- or cutting-grown.

Flowering & pollination Spring. Self-fertile.

Harvesting Winter to spring. Most citrus store well on tree and become sweeter with time. Mandarins must be picked when ripe. Some citrus bear biennially—that is, have heavy crops in alternate years. Pruning is not required for fruit production but can be done in spring to reduce size and remove old wood.

Growing information Keep weed free, fertilise in late winter and late summer, water well when fruit is forming.

ABOVE Oranges can be left on the tree and harvested as needed.

Pests Aphids, bugs, citrus leaf miner, scale, birds, rats.

Diseases Rust, root rot.

CRABAPPLE *See* APPLE

COFFEE *See* CITRUS

CUCUMBER
Cucumis sativus

Family Cucurbitaceae

Other edible plants grown in the same way Beans, Ceylon spinach, choko, melons, sweet potato.

Plant type Annual vine.

Size 2 m+.

Climate & aspect All (best in warm, frost-free areas, protect from cold). Full sun.

ABOVE Cucumbers fruit prolifically. Harvest fruit while young and tender.

Planting Spring to summer (year round in tropics).

Propagation Seed.

Flowering & pollination Spring to summer. Male and female flowers on the same plant. Some commercial varieties have self-fertile female flowers.

Harvesting Harvest small fruit when tender, 8–12 weeks from sowing.

Growing information Dig in organic matter and fertiliser prior to planting. Cucumbers are naturally trailing plants. For ease of harvesting and to keep the fruit away from the ground, train these vines up a tripod or along a trellis or fence. Keep well watered.

Pests Caterpillars, whitefly.

Diseases Powdery mildew.

CUMQUAT *See* CITRUS

ABOVE Eggplants come in many shapes from finger-shaped varieties (shown) to fat globe types. Usually dark purple, there are also white-fruiting varieties.

ABOVE Figs are delicious and sweet when picked fu Water well during summer for large, juicy fruit.

D–E

DAIKON *See* CARROT

EGGPLANT, AUBERGINE
Solanum melongena

Family Solanaceae

Other edible plants grown in the same way Capsicum, potato, tomato.

Plant type Shrubby annual.

Size 90 cm x 60 cm.

Climate & aspect All. Full sun.

Planting Spring to summer in temperate climates, late spring to early summer in cold climates (year round in tropics).

Propagation Seed or seedlings.

Flowering & pollination Spring to autumn. Self-fertile.

Harvesting 14–16 weeks.

Growing information In cold areas start plants in punnets and plant out as weather warms. Grow in rich, well-drained soil. Plants may need staking in exposed areas. Water regularly.

Pests Aphids, bugs, 28-spotted or leaf-eating ladybirds.

Diseases Few.

ENDIVE *See* LETTUCE

ENGLISH SPINACH
See LETTUCE

F

FIG
Ficus carica

Family Moraceae

Other edible plants grown in the same way Mulberry.

Plant type Deciduous tree.

Size 10 m x 4.5 m (generally smaller in cultivation).

Climate & aspect All (best with long, dry summer). Full sun.

Planting Winter (bare-rooted). Spring to summer (potted).

Propagation Aerial layering, cuttings.

ABOVE The roots of ginger are harvested in autumn. Save part of the crop for replanting. Grow in rich, well-drained soil.

Flowering & pollination Spring to autumn. Self-fertile varieties available. Species figs require the fig wasp for pollination.

Harvesting Late summer to autumn. A small or 'breba' crop is produced in spring.

Growing information Grow as a free-standing tree (can be espaliered against a wall in cold climates). Plant into well-drained soil with added compost. Fertilise in spring and early autumn with organic fertiliser for fruiting plants. Water deeply during summer for large, juicy fruit.

Pests Birds, fruit fly, scale.

Diseases Rust.

FRUIT SALAD PLANT
See PASSIONFRUIT

G

GALANGAL *See* GINGER

GARLIC *See* ONION

GINGER
Zingiber officinale

Family Zingiberaceae

Other edible plants grown in the same way Other members of the ginger family including cardamom, galangal or Thai ginger; bamboo, Jerusalem artichoke, lemongrass, turmeric.

Plant type Perennial.

Size 1 m x 1 m.

Climate & aspect All, but best in tropics and subtropics. Full sun to part shade.

Planting The roots of ginger are harvested in autumn. Save part of the crop for replanting.

Propagation Seed or seedlings.

Flowering & pollination Summer, any time in tropics. Most varieties are sterile.

Harvesting 20 weeks or more depending on climate zone.

Growing information Plant in spring and harvest in autumn or winter. Grow in rich, well-drained soil. Mulch with well-rotted manure. Water when dry. Cut back in cool zones when stems die down in winter.

Pests Few.

Diseases Few.

GLOBE ARTICHOKE
See ARTICHOKE

GOOSEBERRY
See BRAMBLES

GOURD *See* PUMPKIN

GRAPE
Vitis vinifera

Family Vitaceae

Other edible plants grown in the same way Kiwifruit.

Plant type Deciduous vine.

Size 10 m x 4.5 m (smaller with pruning).

Climate & aspect All. Full sun.

Planting Winter when dormant, or any time from pots.

Propagation Cutting, grafting.

Flowering & pollination Spring. Bee-pollinated.

Harvesting Late summer to autumn (tropical plantings crop winter to spring).

Growing information Grow in well-drained soil. Mulch with well-rotted manure and fertilise in spring as new growth begins. Water when dry. Train on to a trellis, fence or pergola. Net to protect from birds (see 'Crop protection', page 58). Prune shard in winter.

Pests Birds, caterpillars, scale.

Diseases Phylloxera (movement of vines in grape-growing regions prohibited), powdery mildew, rust.

ABOVE Don't let the birds beat you to your grapes harvest. Net or bag fruit.

GRAPEFRUIT *See* CITRUS

J–K

JERUSALEM ARTICHOKE
See GINGER

KALE *See* BEETROOT

KIWIFRUIT, CHINESE GOOSEBERRY
Actinidia deliciosa

Family Actinidiaceae

Other edible plants grown in the same way Grape.

Plant type Deciduous vine.

Size 10 m x 10 m (but kept smaller with pruning).

ABOVE Male and female kiwifruit plants are needed for fruit production on female plants.

Climate & aspect All but tropics. Full sun.

Planting Winter when dormant, or any time from pots.

Propagation Cuttings, grafting.

Flowering & pollination Spring. Bee-pollinated. Male and female flowers on separate plants; one male needed for up to eight female plants.

Harvesting Autumn and winter.

Growing information Grow in well-drained soil. Mulch with well-rotted manure and fertilise in spring as new growth begins. Water when dry. Train on to a trellis, fence or pergola. Prune hard in winter.

Pests Birds.

Diseases Few.

KOHL RABI *See* BEETROOT

KUMARA *See* CEYLON SPINACH

L

LEEK
Allium ampeloprasum var. *porrum* / *A. porrum*

Family Alliaceae

Other edible plants grown in the same way Shallots, spring onion.

Plant type Grown as an annual.

Size 30 cm x 15 cm.

Climate & aspect All. Full sun.

Planting Spring to autumn (temperate to cold climates), late summer to autumn in subtropical and tropical climates.

Propagation Seed (sown in seed trays), seedlings.

Flowering & pollination Harvest before flowering.

Harvesting 12–20 weeks (from when stems are 2 cm diameter).

Growing information Grow in well–drained soil. Plant seedlings into individual 10–15 cm deep holes or trench 20 cm deep and cover with soil as plants grow. Water and fertilise regularly for quick growth.

Pests Aphids.

Diseases Few.

LEMON *See* CITRUS

LEMONGRASS *See* GINGER

LEMON MYRTLE *See* BAY TREE

LETTUCE
Lactuca sativa

Family Asteraceae

Other edible plants grown in the same way Asian greens, endive, English spinach, pak choi, rocket.

Plant type Annual.

Size 30 cm x 30 cm.

Climate & aspect All. Full sun to part shade (especially in hot zones and during summer in warm areas).

Planting All year.

Propagation Seed, seedlings.

Flowering & pollination Harvest before flowering.

Harvesting 8–12 weeks. Harvest leaves of loose-leaved varieties as needed.

Growing information Grow in well–drained soil with added organic matter. Shade new seedlings in hot weather. Encourage quick growth with regular watering (daily or twice daily in summer) and fortnightly applications of liquid fertiliser.

Pests Caterpillars, snails, slugs.

Diseases Fungal diseases.

LEMON GRASS *See* GINGER

LILLYPILLY *See* CITRUS

LIME *See* CITRUS

BELOW Leeks are related to onions but grown for their thick white stems.

BELOW Lettuce can be grown in rows or tucked into spaces between other crops.

M

MACADAMIA
Macadamia integrifolia,
M. tetraphylla

Family Proteaceae

Other edible plants grown in the same way Other evergreen tree nuts, tropical fruiting trees.

Plant type Evergreen tree.

Size 12 m x 6 m (smaller in cultivation).

Climate & aspect All. Full sun to part shade.

Planting Any time.

BELOW Macadamia fruit has a green outer skin and hard brown inner skin.

Propagation Seed, cutting or grafting (for named varieties).

Flowering & pollination Spring. Bee-pollinated.

Harvesting Late summer to autumn (fruit drops when mature).

Growing information Grow in well-drained soil. Mulch with organic matter and fertilise in spring with low-phosphorus fertiliser. Water when dry. Prune to maintain tree size.

Pests Rats, nut borers.

Diseases Root rot.

MANDARIN *See* CITRUS

MANGO *See* CITRUS

MARJORAM *See* BASIL

MARROW *See* PUMPKIN

MEDLAR *See* APPLE

MELONS *See* CUCUMBER

MINT *See* BASIL

MONSTERA DELICIOSA
See PASSIONFRUIT

MULBERRY *See* FIG

MUSTARD *See* BEETROOT

N–O

NECTARINE *See* PEACH

NEW ZEALAND SPINACH
See CEYLON SPINACH

OKRA *See* ROSELLA

OLIVE
Olea europaea

Family Oleaceae

Other edible plants grown in the same way Persimmon.

Plant type Evergreen tree.

Size 6–9 m x 6 m.

Climate & aspect Cool to temperate. Full sun.

Planting All year round (but best in late winter to spring). Select named varieties (some olive varieties are preferred for fruit, others for oil).

Propagation Cuttings, suckers, potted plants.

Flowering & pollination Spring. Bee-pollinated. Self-fertile but crops may be better when flowers are cross-pollinated.

Harvesting Autumn to early winter when full and purple. Ripe olives are bitter and must be processed before they are eaten by soaking first in water then in brine. Change water daily for 10 days then transfer olives to brine (1 cup of salt to 4 cups of water) and allow to soak for a further 3–4 weeks. Olives are ready when they no longer taste bitter. Discard soft olives. From this stage they can be eaten, cooked or stored in brine or oil.

Growing information Grow olives in well-drained, slightly alkaline soil. Drought hardy once established, but crops better with regular watering especially through spring and summer. Prune in winter after harvest to control size or remove damaged or crossing branches. Control weeds by hoeing regularly between the rows.

Pests Scale.

Diseases Few.

ONION
Allium cepa

Family Alliaceae

Other edible plants grown in the same way Garlic, spring onions, shallots.

Plant type Biennial bulb grown as an annual.

Size 30–60 cm x 20 cm.

Climate & aspect All. Full sun.

Planting Autumn to spring. Plant early, mid and late maturing varieties according to season.

Propagation Seed, seedlings, or immature bulbs (called sets).

Flowering & pollination Spring. Bee-pollinated.

Harvesting 6–8 months (harvest when tops dry and fall over).

Growing information Grow in well-drained soil that has been enriched before planting with bonemeal or pelletised organic fertiliser. Neutral pH is preferred so add garden lime or dolomite to acidic soils. Do not plant deeply (plant seedlings or sets 1 cm deep and 15 cm apart in rows that are 40 cm apart as bulbs sit on surface). Control weeds. Water when dry and feed regularly as bulbs are forming.

Pests Aphids.

Diseases Root rot.

ORANGE *See* CITRUS

OREGANO *See* BASIL

BELOW Olives thrive in Mediterranean climates and need well-drained soils.

BELOW Don't plant onions too deeply. Harvest bulbs by pulling up entire plant after flowering as the tops die off.

P

PAK CHOI *See* LETTUCE

PAPAYA *See* PAWPAW

PARSLEY *See* BASIL

PARSNIP *See* CARROT

PASSIONFRUIT
Passiflora edulis

Family Passifloraceae

Other edible plants grown in the same way *Monstera deliciosa* (fruit salad plant).

Plant type Evergreen vine.

Size 12 m x 6 m (smaller in cultivation).

Climate & aspect All (except coldest areas). Full sun.

Planting All year.

Propagation Seed, grafting (for named varieties).

Flowering & pollination Spring to autumn. Bee-pollinated. Some varieties require cross-pollination.

Harvesting Late summer to autumn when vines are 18 months or more old.

Growing information Grow in well-drained soil with added organic matter including well-rotted manure. Mulch with organic matter and fertilise in spring and late summer. Water regularly when fruit is forming. Prune overgrown vines in spring to open up fruit to sunlight.

ABOVE Passionfruit vines don't begin to fruit until 12–18 months of age.

Pests Passionfruit leafhopper, possums, rats.

Diseases Virus.

PAWPAW
Carica papaya

Family Caricaceae

Other edible plants grown in the same way Babaco, banana.

Plant type Herbaceous tree.

Size 6 m x 3 m (some dwarf forms available).

Climate & aspect All. Full sun to part shade.

Planting All year.

ABOVE Pawpaw needs a warm, frost-free climate for good growth.

Propagation Seed, suckers.

Flowering & pollination Male, female and self-fertile plants (eliminate most male plants).

Harvesting Fruit takes 6–12 months to mature (colours to orange when ripe).

Growing information Grow in rich, well-drained soil. Mulch with organic matter and fertilise regularly. Water regularly. Shelter from wind and frost. Prune after fruiting and encourage new suckers to replace the stem that has fruited. Renew clumps every five years or as vigour declines. Grow pawpaws in nutrient-enriched, well-drained soil.

Pests Bats, possums, rats.

Diseases Virus and bacterial.

PEACH
Prunus persica

Family Rosaceae

Other edible plants grown in the same way Almond, cherry, nectarine, plum.

Plant type Deciduous tree.

Size 3 m x 3 m (dwarf varieties available).

Climate & aspect Cold to subtropics (low-chill varieties in warm-winter climates). Full sun.

Planting Winter (bare-rooted), all year for potted plants.

Propagation Grafting (for named varieties).

Flowering & pollination Winter to spring. Bee-pollinated. Some varieties need cross-pollination.

Harvesting Summer to autumn.

Growing information Grow in well-drained soil. Mulch with organic matter and fertilise in spring. Water when dry, especially when fruit is forming. Prune after harvest in autumn to encourage new growth and to maintain tree size.

Pests Birds, fruit fly.

Diseases Peach leaf curl, fungal diseases.

PEANUT
Arachis hypogaea

Family Fabaceae

Other edible plants grown in the same way Peas, beans and other legumes.

Plant type Annual grown as a low bush or groundcover.

ABOVE Peach trees flower before the leaves appear with fruit developing as the weather warms.

Size 50 cm x 1 m.

Climate & aspect Temperate to tropics (need a warm growing season). Full sun.

Planting Spring (all year in tropical areas).

Propagation Seed (removed from pod but with papery covering intact).

Flowering & pollination Late spring to summer. Self-pollinating. Once flowers are fertilised the stems (known as pegs) bend down to bury their tips in the soil. The pod bearing the peanuts then develops 5–10 cm below ground.

Harvesting Summer to autumn (year round in tropical areas), 120–150 days from planting (9–10 weeks after the peg penetrates the soil). In cold or frost-prone regions with a short summer growing

ABOVE Peanuts are a fun crop to grow. Their roots also enrich nitrogen-poor soils.

season peanuts can be harvested after the tops have died off as they continue to mature underground. Cut roots and remove entire plant to harvest nuts. Dry the plant after it is pulled up and before harvesting nuts (for at least three weeks but no longer than three months). Discard mouldy nuts as they are toxic.

Growing information Grow in well-drained, light soil. Add gypsum or calcium to soil before planting. Water when dry (peanuts grow best with regular moisture). Peanuts can be grown as a green manure crop as they add nitrogen to soils. Keep weed free by hoeing regularly between the rows.

Pests Aphids, weevils.

Diseases Fungus (aflatoxin).

PEAR *See* APPLE

PEAS
Pisum sativum

Family Fabaceae

Other edible plants grown in the same way All peas, including climbing peas, bush peas, snow peas, sugar snaps.

Plant type Annual climber.

Size 2 m x 2 m.

Climate & aspect All. Full sun to part shade.

Planting Autumn to spring (warmer season plantings in cool zones only).

Propagation Seed (direct sown), seedlings.

Flowering & pollination Spring. Self-fertile.

Harvesting 12–16 weeks (snow peas from 8 weeks).

Growing information Train climbing forms on to a teepee or trellis. Grow in well-drained soil with added organic matter. Mulch with organic matter and fertilise regularly in as pods set. Water regularly.

Pests Aphids, caterpillars.

Diseases Powdery mildew.

PERSIMMON *See* OLIVE

PINEAPPLE
Ananas comosus

Family Bromeliaceae

Other edible plants grown in the same way None.

Plant type Short-lived perennial.

Size 1.5 m x 1 m.

Climate & aspect Tropics, subtropics, warm temperate (in a cool or temperate climate a conservatory or winter covering is needed to protect the plant from damage). Full sun to part shade.

Planting All year. Can be grown in pots in cold climates.

Propagation Pineapple top, basal offset.

Flowering & pollination Any time. Self-fertile.

Harvesting Fruit takes 6 months to 2 years to ripen. Fruit changes colour to orange with maturity.

BELOW Peas are a cool climate crop fruiting through winter and spring.

BELOW Pineapples are a form of bromeliad that thrive in the tropics and subtropics. The fruit takes up to 2 years to ripen.

Growing information Grow in well-drained soil (raised beds are ideal). Mulch and fertilise after planting and then every 8–12 weeks. Liquid feed is ideal. These plants do not require extra watering.

Pests Few.

Diseases Few.

PLANTAIN *See* BANANA

PLUM *See* APRICOT

POMEGRANATE *See* CITRUS

POTATO
Solanum tuberosum

Family Solanaceae

Other edible plants grown in the same way Other Solanaceae (tomato, capsicum, chillies, etc.) and root vegetables.

Plant type Annual tuber.

Size 60 cm x 45 cm.

Climate & aspect All. Full sun.

Planting Late winter to summer, autumn in warm climates (avoid summer plantings in tropical climates). Plants are frost sensitive.

Propagation Tubers (known as seed potatoes). *Note*: Grow certified virus-free tubers.

Flowering & pollination Spring.

Harvesting 16–20 weeks. Small new potatoes can be dug 3 weeks after flowering but tubers can be left in the ground to mature.

Growing information Grow in well-drained soil. Plant seed potatoes, or sections each with at least one eye or sprout. Allow tubers or eyes to sprout before planting. Plant in furrow 15 cm deep. Lightly cover, then hill up soil around potatoes as they grow (tubers exposed to light develop greening which can be toxic). Keep free of weeds. Potatoes are frost sensitive.

Pests Aphids, bugs, caterpillars, root knot nematode, wireworms.

Diseases Potato blight, rot (including black leg, gangrene), scab.

PUMPKIN
Cucurbita maxima

Family Cucurbitaceae

Other edible plants grown in the same way Gourd, marrow, squash, zucchini.

Plant type Annual vine.

BELOW Potatoes are grown from small tubers called seed potatoes.

Size 50 cm x 3 m (bush varieties available).

Climate & aspect All. Full sun.

Planting Spring.

Propagation Seed.

Flowering & pollination Spring to summer. Bee-pollinated. Male and female flowers on same plant.

Harvesting Late summer to autumn (after frost in cold zones).

Growing information Grow in rich, well-drained soil with added organic matter. Mulch well and fertilise in spring. Water when dry. Long laterals can be tip-pruned to control spread and to encourage lateral branching and the production of female flowers.

Pests Bugs, rats.

Diseases Powdery mildew.

BELOW 'Golden Nugget' is a compact bush variety of pumpkin.

Q–R

QUINCE *See* APPLE

RADISH *See* CARROT

RASPBERRY *See* BRAMBLES

RHUBARB
Rheum x hybridum)

Family Polygonaceae

Other edible plants grown in the same way Silverbeet.

Plant type Perennial.

Size 90 cm x 1 m.

Climate & aspect All. Full sun to part shade.

Planting All year, but best in late winter.

Propagation Crowns.

Flowering & pollination Remove flowers if they appear.

Harvesting 8–12 weeks from planting. Plants crop year round and leaves can be harvested when they are growing vigorously and the crown is producing plenty of stems.

Growing information Grow in well-drained soil enriched with organic matter. Fertilise in spring and as young leaves form. Water plants regularly as may bolt if drought stressed. Harvest outer leaves by twisting off at base. Eat only stalks (cooked), discard leaves into compost. Leaves contain high levels of oxalates which can be poisonous.

ABOVE Thick red rhubarb stems are prized by cooks, but green varieties are also grown.

Pests Snails.

Diseases Crown rot.

ROCKET
See **LETTUCE**

ROCKMELON
See **CUCUMBER**

ROSELLA
Hibiscus sabdariffa

Family Malvaceae

Other edible plants grown in the same way Okra.

Plant type Shrub grown as annual or biennial.

Size 2 m x 2 m.

ABOVE The unopened buds of the rosella plant are used for jam and preserves.

Climate & aspect Subtropics to tropics (and warm coastal areas in temperate climates). Full sun to part shade.

Planting Spring (dry season in tropical zones).

Propagation Seed.

Flowering & pollination Summer to autumn. Self-fertile.

Harvesting 6 months after planting.

Growing information Grow in rich, well-drained soil. Mulch with organic matter and fertilise in spring. Water when dry.

Pests Bugs.

Diseases Few.

ROSEMARY *See* BAY TREE

S

SAGE *See* BASIL

SHALLOT *See* ONION

SILVERBEET *See* RHUBARB

SNOW PEA *See* PEAS

SPRING ONION *See* CHIVES

SQUASH *See* PUMPKIN

STRAWBERRY
Fragaria x *ananassa*

Family Rosaceae

Other edible plants grown in the same way None.

Plant type Perennial groundcover.

Size 15 cm x 90 cm.

Climate & aspect All. Full sun.

Planting Autumn to winter.

Propagation Virus-free plants, runners.

Flowering & pollination Late winter to summer. Self-fertile. Bee-pollinated.

Harvesting Spring to autumn (some varieties are day-length sensitive).

Growing information Grow in fertile soil with added organic matter. Control weeds. Fertilise when fruiting. Keep well watered. Use organic mulch such as straw

ABOVE Strawberries are part of the rose family and thrive with added nutrients and mulching.

or pine needles to conserve moisture and protect fruit from fungal disease.

Pests Birds, snails, slugs.

Diseases Grey mould.

SWEDE *See* BEETROOT

SWEET CORN
Zea mays

Family Poaceae

Other edible plants grown in the same way None.

Plant type Annual grass.

Size 2–3 m x 1 m.

Climate & aspect All. Full sun.

ABOVE Sweet corn cobs taste best when freshly harvested and cooked.

Planting Spring (all year in tropics).

Propagation Seed (direct sown).

Flowering & pollination Spring to autumn. Self-fertile. Wind-pollinated.

Harvesting 12–16 weeks. Cobs are plump and kernels filled with milky juice.

Growing information Plant in blocks of at least 1 m square to aid pollination. Grow in rich, fertile soil with added organic fertiliser (keep seed out of direct contact with fertiliser). Control weeds. Fertilise when flowering. Keep well watered especially in hot weather. Poor pollination leads to cobs forming without kernels. This occurs where corn is not planted in blocks or where caterpillars have damaged the male flowers.

Pests Caterpillars.

Diseases Damping off.

SWEET POTATO
Ipomoea batatas

Family Convolvulaceae

Other edible plants grown in the same way Taro, yam.

Plant type Biennial vine usually grown as an annual groundcover.

Size 2–3 m x 3 m.

Climate & aspect Tropical to temperate. Full sun.

Planting Spring (tubers), late spring to summer (tip cuttings). All year in tropics. Let tubers shoot then divide before planting.

Propagation Tubers, tip cuttings.

Flowering & pollination Summer to autumn. Self-fertile (but grown for underground tubers).

Harvesting 16–20 weeks as foliage begins to yellow.

Growing information Plant in rich, well-drained soil. Mulch to control weeds. Keep well watered during summer. In cooler areas grow a single tuber in a large (50 cm diameter) pot. Vine can be trained up a teepee in a small space.

Pests Caterpillars, weevils.

Diseases Shot hole (fungal disease).

BELOW Sweet potato needs a long growing season that's free of frost. Plant in rich, well-drained soil and mulch to control weeds.

T

TAMARILLO, TREE TOMATO
Solanum betaceum

Family Solanaceae

Other edible plants grown in the same way Tomato, other tropical fruit trees.

Plant type Evergreen tree or shrub.

Size 3 m x 2 m.

Climate & aspect All. Full sun to part shade. Wind protection.

BELOW Tamarillos are part of the tomato family but form a small tree.

Planting Spring (all year in tropics).

Propagation Cutting, potted plant.

Flowering & pollination Spring to autumn. Self-fertile.

Harvesting Spring to autumn. Fruit ripens to deep red (some varieties have golden or orange fruit).

Growing information Grow tamarillos in rich, well-drained soil. Dig in compost and well-rotted manure before planting. Prune if necessary to encourage single trunk. Mulch heavily and water regularly especially when dry.

Pests Birds, caterpillars, flying fox, snails.

Diseases Root rot.

TANGERINE *See* CITRUS

TARO *See* SWEET POTATO

TEA *See* CITRUS

TOMATO
Lycopersicon esculentum

Family Solanaceae

Other edible plants grown in the same way Capsicum, chilli, eggplant, tree tomato.

Plant type Annual vine.

Size 2 m x 60 cm (dwarf and cascading varieties available).

Climate & aspect All. Full sun.

Planting Spring to summer.

ABOVE Tomatoes are delicious when harvested sun-ripened from home-grown vines. Stake to avoid damage and to better manage the crop.

Propagation Seed, seedlings, grafted.

Flowering & pollination Spring to summer (year round in subtropical and tropical zones). Self-fertile. Flowering reduced when temperatures exceed 35° C.

Harvesting Spring to autumn (year round in warm climates).

Growing information Grow in rich, fertile soil with added organic matter. Fertilise when flowering and fruiting with a pelletised organic or liquid plant food. Keep well watered. Mulch to conserve moisture. Stake to avoid damage and to better manage crop. Remove laterals to control size.

Pests Birds, caterpillars, fruit fly.

Diseases Blossom end rot (calcium deficiency), fungus, virus.

TURMERIC *See* GINGER

TURNIP *See* BEETROOT

W–Z

WATERMELON
See CUCUMBER

YAM *See* SWEET POTATO

ZUCCHINI
See PUMPKIN

CHAPTER 11

A–Z of pests, diseases and other garden problems

Why do I need to read this chapter?

How to use this guide

Insect pests and diseases are part and parcel of gardening. Sometimes pests can be tolerated, but at other times they need to be removed if a plant is going to survive or at least produce flowers or fruit.

However, control of both pests and diseases in an organic garden can be problematic as many recommended control methods, such as chemical sprays, do not fit into an organic gardening system.

In these pages you will find some of the most common pests and diseases identified with information on how to control them by organically friendly means. The appropriate chemical controls are also listed, but should only be used with care and consideration—and never on plants whose crops are to be sold. Always follow the instructions on product labels especially relating to rates and timing of application.

Pests and diseases

This A–Z is divided into three sections: insect pests, diseases and deficiencies. Identify the type of problem you have (see page 114 for how to distinguish between insect pest and disease) and then consult the A–Z guide for more details on the problem affecting your plant.

Although there are many pests and diseases, only the main types you are likely to encounter are dealt with here; these control methods can also be used for less commonly seen pests and diseases that affect plants in similar ways to the more common ones.

Correct identification

Insect pests damage plants by attacking all parts of their growth—from roots to shoots, trunks, leaves, fruit and flowers. Examine affected plants carefully, using a magnifying glass if necessary, to identify the pest that is causing the problem.

Sometimes the insect you see is not the problem. For example, the small spiders and wasps often found in and on plants are unlikely to be causing damage. Indeed, most are beneficial insects to be encouraged and appreciated in organic gardens.

LEFT Mealy bug is a serious pest problem. It attacks all parts of the plant including the roots and can be very difficult to defeat.

Pests

ANTS

Many types of ants are encountered in gardens. While ants play an important role in breaking down material, they can cause problems both for the gardener and the plants. Ants may bite, and some can be very dangerous—among them the introduced yellow crazy ant (*Anoplolepis gracilipes*), the introduced South American fire ant (*Solenopsis invicta*) and the Australian jumping ant (*Myrmecia pilosula*), a species of bull ant. The presence of any of these pest ants should be reported immediately to your local Department of Agriculture, as their control is mandatory. Other species of ants 'farm' some sap-sucking pests such as aphids and scale, moving them from plant to plant and deterring natural predators. Ants can also make nests in pots, which are detrimental to the welfare of the potted plants.

Active season Active throughout the year but may be more obvious when it is wet.

Plants affected Citrus trees, roses, but also found on many other plants.

Control methods
PHYSICAL Exclude ants from trees, shrubs and pot plants with sticky barriers; use water as a moat to prevent ants getting access to pet dishes and pots; boiling water poured down ant nests can get rid of ants in paved outdoor living areas.

BIOCONTROL Echidnas eat ants.

CHEMICAL Sprinkle borax or make a bait by mixing it with sugar and water. Keep the mixture away from pets and children. Other chemical controls include pyrethrum. Non-organic controls include ant sand.

Comment
Not to be confused with white ants (correctly called termites), which damage timber in gardens and structures. If termites are discovered, call a qualified pest controller.

APHIDS

Aphids are also referred to as 'green fly'. There are many species of aphids and many are found only on specific host plants. These small, soft-bodied insects are green, brown or black and reproduce quickly, giving birth to live young. They suck sap from new growth and can spread virus diseases. Mature aphids have wings.

Active season Year round, but particularly in spring on new growth.

Preferred hosts Found in large numbers on new growth, particularly on roses, citrus, peach trees and brassicas.

BELOW Ants invade dry ground but also colonise trees and shrubs.

Control methods
PHYSICAL Sticky boards available from organic suppliers or nurseries, hosing off new growth, squashing.

BIOCONTROLS Aphids are eaten by ladybirds and their larvae, and some species are parasitised by wasps. Predators including ladybirds and the rose wasp (*Aphidius rosae*) are available in commercial quantities. Small birds such as silvereyes also feed on aphids on garden plants. Avoid using any chemicals where biological controls are active.

CHEMICAL CONTROLS Most garden chemicals, including homemade soap and garlic sprays, soap sprays, spinosad, pyrethrum and oil sprays kill aphids.

Comment
Control ants as part of aphid control. Sooty mould (see page 177) is associated with aphid activity.

BELOW Aphids suck sap and can spread viral diseases to plants.

BUGS

Many garden pests are known as 'bugs'. Bugs are identified by having long feelers and a distinct waist. They include ladybirds, hoppers, green vegetable bugs, spined citrus bugs and bronze orange bugs (usually called stink bugs). These insects hatch from eggs often laid in or around host plants and mature through several juvenile stages before reaching their adult form. Control is easiest against juvenile bugs.

Active season Some bugs are active year round, but most are seen in spring and summer.

Plants affected An extensive range of productive and ornamental plants. Citrus trees are attacked by spined citrus bugs and bronze orange bugs. Many vegetables are attacked by green vegetable bugs, pest ladybirds (including the 1 cm long orange and black 26- or 28-spotted ladybird) and hoppers such as leaf hoppers found on passionfruit.

Control methods

PHYSICAL Squash any bugs you catch; also look for and squash egg clusters. Take care, as some bugs exude an irritating liquid that can damage the eyes.

BIOCONTROLS Many pest bugs warn off birds and other would-be predators with their bright colours, so biocontrols are very limited in effect.

CHEMICAL Bugs are resistant to many garden chemicals. Horticultural oils may be used to smother their breathing apparatus when they are in a juvenile life stage. Pyrethrum sprays can also be used.

Comment

Bugs can chew foliage and their larvae may chew roots, however not all bugs are bad. Assassin bugs are predators that control a wide range of pest insects including caterpillars, spiders and snails. Ladybirds (both adults and young) are excellent garden predators particularly against aphids.

CATERPILLARS

Caterpillars are the larvae of butterflies and moths. Unlike the adults, which feed on nectar, caterpillars eat leaves and flowers. Many are serious pests of vegetables. Of note is the green caterpillar seen on brassicas, which turns into the cabbage white butterfly.

Active season Caterpillars can be active throughout the year but are most damaging between spring and autumn.

Plants affected Most plants can be attacked by caterpillars but particularly keep an eye on all brassicas and mint (leaves), gardenias (leaves), tomatoes (fruit) and sweet corn (cobs).

Control methods

PHYSICAL Squash any caterpillars found. Strong, healthy plants may be able to outgrow caterpillars.

BELOW This green vegetable bug is laying its eggs on a stem. They also lay eggs on the underside of leaves. Learn to recognise the eggs of this and other pest species. Squash eggs to reduce pest numbers.

BELOW Caterpillars damage leaves, flowers and fruit but turn into moths or butterflies.

BIOCONTROLS Wasps and small birds, and domestic poultry including guinea fowl, are effective caterpillar controls.

CHEMICAL Bt, sold as Dipel, is an organic insecticide based on *Bacillus thuringiensis* that attacks the stomachs of caterpillars that become moths and butterflies. Spinosad (derived from a soil bacterium) kills caterpillars on contact and after feeding on sprayed foliage. Products containing azadirachtin (neem), an extract from the neem tree are also registered against chewing insects such as caterpillars and suited to organic gardening methods.

Comment
Some creatures that resemble caterpillars are the larvae of sawflies. These can be squashed or trapped but do not respond to Bt as they do not turn into moths or butterflies.

CODLING MOTH

The larvae (caterpillars) of this serious pest of pome fruit tunnel into the developing fruit and feed in the core.

Active season Late spring and summer. Larvae enter the fruit as it is forming.

Plants affected Apple, pear and quince trees.

Control methods
PHYSICAL Band trees with sticky bands made by applying a band of grease or a commercially available product, or wrap corrugated cardboard around the trunk to prevent larvae from reaching pupating sites under the bark. In winter, check loose bark and kill any pupae found. Remove damaged fruit.

BIOCONTROLS Pheromone traps attract and kill adult males. Trichogramma wasps parasitise eggs of the moth. Attract beneficial insects such as wasps by

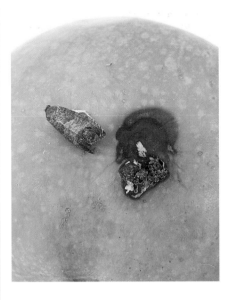

ABOVE The larvae of this codling moth damage pome fruit such as apples and pears.

planting herbs and flowering plants in orchards. Use poultry or grazing animals such as sheep to clean up fallen fruit.

CHEMICAL Difficult to control without using systemic insecticides once the larvae have entered fruit. Codling moth larvae feed briefly on leaves before entering fruit and are vulnerable to insecticides including Bt and spinosad at this stage.

Comment
Affected fruit cannot be stored.

CURL GRUBS

These witchetty grub-like insects, found in soil and potting mix, are the larvae of various beetles including African lawn beetles. They feed on plant roots, weakening or killing plants outright.

Active season Beetles emerge in spring and summer. Curl grubs are found in soil throughout the year.

ABOVE Curl grubs are the larval stage of many beetles. They feed on roots.

Plants affected Potted plants and lawns are particularly affected.

Control methods
PHYSICAL Remove larvae from soil and potting mix. Turn off outside lights to avoid attracting beetles, which lay their eggs in soil, heaps of potting mix or pots.

BIOCONTROLS Wet soils in spring may kill grubs. Bandicoots, magpies and foraging poultry dig up grubs and eat them. Birds and other animals also eat adult beetles.

CHEMICAL Azadirachtin (neem) is registered for curl grub control. Drenches based on tea tree and eucalyptus oil are effective. Imidacloprid is registered as a soil drench but is not suited for organic gardening. There are also chemical controls for beetles.

Comment
Beetles favour dry soil conditions and often prosper in times of drought.

ABOVE The earwigs that damage flowers and foliage are an introduced pest, however, some native species are beneficial. Pest species are readily identified by their pincer-like appendage.

ABOVE Fruit fly pierce the skin of ripening fruit as they lay eggs.

EARWIGS

These small brown insects are easily recognised by the pair of forceps-like pincers extending from the abdomen. They feed on pollen and also eat flower petals and leaves.

Active season Spring and summer.

Plants affected Many flowering plants.

Control methods
PHYSICAL Trap and kill pests. Make traps from upturned pots stuffed with newspaper. Fish oil is highly attractive to earwigs and can be used to bait traps. Empty traps daily to remove pest.

BIOCONTROLS None commercially available.

CHEMICAL As earwigs feed inside flowers and hide during the day they are difficult to control with chemicals. Systemic sprays registered for control are not suited to organic gardening.

Comment
Some native earwigs are predators and are beneficial in gardens.

FRUIT FLIES

Queensland and Mediterranean fruit flies are pests of soft fruits in parts of Australia. Tasmania, Victoria and South Australia are free of fruit fly. The female lays eggs in fruit. After hatching, the larvae cause damage as they feed inside the fruit. Affected fruit rots and falls from the tree.

Active season Summer and early autumn. In warm climates fruit fly may be active from late winter.

Plants affected All soft fruits, including tomato and capsicum. Small-fruited tomatoes such as cherry tomatoes are not usually attacked.

Control methods
PHYSICAL Protect fruit with exclusion bags or nets. Grow early season fruits that ripen before fruit fly is active. Harvest fruit before it ripens and complete ripening indoors (this is effective with tomatoes). Gather infested fruit, place it in a sealed plastic bag and allow the bag to stew in the sun for a week to kill maggots. Dispose of in a rubbish bin or bury.

BIOCONTROLS Fruit fly traps, baited with a pheromone, attract male flies and are an indicator of fly activity.

CHEMICAL Splash baits contain a protein and an insecticide (spinosad). The protein attracts the female to feed while the insecticide she ingests kills her before she lays any eggs. This bait works as female fruit fly require a feed of protein before they can lay eggs.

Comment
Quarantine restrictions preventing the transport of fruit into Victoria, South Australia and Tasmania are designed to stop the spread of fruit fly into fruit fly-free zones.

GRASSHOPPERS

Grasshoppers, locusts, leaf hoppers and katydids can be present in plague proportions and chew foliage and flowers. They are often active at night. Large numbers can strip crops bare. They both fly and hop to avoid predators.

Active season May appear at any time but are particularly associated with the warm weather of spring and summer.

Plants affected Any plant can be attacked but particularly grasses, grains, roses and tropical foliage plants.

Control methods

PHYSICAL Catch and kill individuals (grasshoppers are often easiest to catch in the cool of the morning). Net badly damaged foliage to allow regrowth.

BIOCONTROLS Green Guard® is a biological control against grasshoppers and locusts developed by the CSIRO. Birds, including poultry, and reptiles—particularly lizards—help control grasshoppers, leaf hoppers and katydids.

CHEMICAL Some contact and systemic chemicals are registered against grasshoppers but are not suited to organic gardening.

Comment

Grasshoppers and locusts are extremely damaging in broadacre farming.

LEAF MINERS

The larvae of flies and other insects that feed inside foliage, leaving silvery trails in the leaf, are called leaf miners. These insects can cause leaves to be distorted. Leaf miners rarely kill plants but can slow growth and the damage they cause is unsightly.

Active season Throughout the year.

Plants affected Citrus, parsley, cineraria, nasturtium, stock and other ornamentals. Lillypillies are affected by a leaf gall.

Control methods

PHYSICAL Remove affected leaves and shoots and destroy them.

BIOCONTROLS None commercially available.

CHEMICAL Horticultural oils sprayed on new citrus growth inhibit female citrus leaf miners laying eggs. Azadirachtin (neem) is registered against citrus leaf miner. Systemic insecticides to kill larvae inside leaf tissue are not compatible with strict organic gardening practices.

Comment

Encouraging new growth with good horticultural practices such as tip pruning, watering and fertilising and then protecting the new growth from attack can drastically reduce the visual impact caused by this pest.

BELOW When they are around in small numbers, grasshoppers can be caught and killed. Swarms, often known as locusts, are highly damaging to crops and pasture.

BELOW Leaf miners tunnel in the tissue of leaves of citrus and cause the leaves to become distorted.

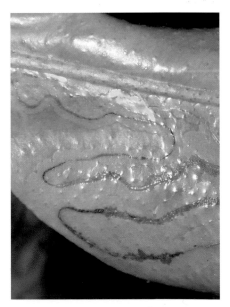

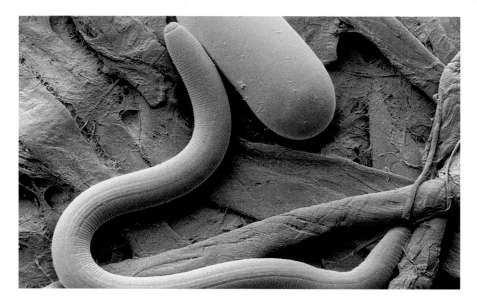

ABOVE Although evident under a microscope, nematodes are not visible to the naked eye. They are recognised by the lumps and swellings that occur when they infest roots.

ABOVE Scale insects are protected by waxy coverings.

NEMATODES

Nematodes are microscopic soil-borne pests, sometimes called root-knot nematodes or eelworms. They infect plant roots causing swellings and nodules that prevent the roots taking up moisture and nutrients, and causing plants to wilt.

Active season Any time.

Plants affected Some plants are more susceptible than others. Tomatoes and potatoes are vulnerable.

Control methods
PHYSICAL Remove affected plants, seal them in a bag, and bin or bury them. Avoid moving soil from infected beds to other areas of the garden. Grow crops that are not attractive to nematodes, including French marigold, mustard and some grasses such as rye.

BIOCONTROLS Some nematodes are not harmful to plants and can be used to control other insect pests. Research is under way to find bacteria that may control nematodes.

CHEMICAL Mustard grown as a green manure crop and dug into soils can release a type of mustard gas that can kill nematodes. Molasses spray can also be used (see page 184). Most soil drenches registered for use against nematodes are not suited to organic gardening methods.

Comment
Pest nematodes are often more severe in sandy soils.

SCALE INSECTS

These sap-sucking insects feed under protective waxy coverings. They vary in size, shape and colour and may be specific to their host plants. They may be large and round or small and narrow, and can be brown, red, pink, black or white. Scale cluster on stems or on leaves. Heavy scale infestations are often a sign that the plant is stressed or growing in unsuitable conditions.

Active season Any time.

Plants affected Most plants can be attacked by scale.

Control methods
PHYSICAL Control ants (see page 165). Improve growing conditions. Prune off badly affected branches.

BIOCONTROLS There are many commercially available biological controls for scale, including ladybirds.

CHEMICAL Use oil sprays to break down the waxy covering and spray with a contact spray such as spinosad or pyrethrum. Copper or lime sprays or washes applied in winter help control scale. Systemic insecticides registered against scale may be required for complete control but these are not suited to organic gardening practices.

Comment

Sooty mould can form on honeydew excreted by scale. See page 177 for more information on controlling sooty mould.

SNAILS AND SLUGS

Snails and slugs feed on foliage, flowers and fruit. They can do severe damage and may kill seedlings.

Active season Any time but particularly after rain periods and at night.

Plants affected All, but seedlings may be killed outright.

Control methods

PHYSICAL Squash or collect and drown in a bucket of salty or soapy water. Trap and dispose. Beer and dog food are attractive to snails and slugs and can be used to bait traps. Copper, grit, coffee grounds and crushed eggshells can be used as barriers around susceptible plants. Snails are often active at night so check vulnerable plants after dark.

BIOCONTROLS Lizards and birds eat snails.

CHEMICAL Caffeine sprays (see page 184), iron-based snail baits. Metaldehyde-based baits are not suited to organic gardening and are toxic to pets and wildlife, including lizards. If baits are used, remove dead and dying snails to avoid secondary poisoning.

Comment

Don't just throw snails over the fence. Recent trials have shown that many can find their way home again.

RIGHT Like snails, slugs are often active at night and after rain. Their presence is shown by silvery trails on the ground. Search for them among foliage.

THRIPS

There are many types of thrips, including western flower thrips, onion thrips and plague thrips, the three types most commonly encountered in gardens. These tiny brown insects infest flowers, often causing flowers to drop early and so reducing crops. They feed on petals, pollen and foliage. They may be present in large numbers, particularly in dry weather.

Active season Spring to autumn.

Plants affected Many plants affected including dahlias and roses.

Control methods
PHYSICAL Cut off affected flowers and put them in a sealed bag in the rubbish or bury them. Yellow sticky traps available from organic suppliers and some nurseries may reduce numbers.

BIOCONTROLS None commercially available.

CHEMICAL Difficult to spray for thrips as the insects are inside flowers. Systemic insecticides registered for use against thrips are not suited to organic gardening. Many thrips are resistant to common pesticides.

Comment
Severe numbers may weaken growth.

TWO-SPOTTED MITE

This tiny pest, about the size of the full stop at the end of this sentence, and yellowish green in colour (in some cold areas it may turn orange or red in winter, which accounts for its other common name of red spider mite), feeds on the undersides of leaves and can severely damage many plants. Silvery leaf discolouration on the top of leaves with webbing and frass (insect droppings) on the underside of the leaves can indicate that mites are active. Examine the underside of affected leaves with a hand lens or magnifying glass to identify this pest. It is often an indication of plant stress and more active in warm, dry conditions.

Active season Any time but particularly in spring and summer.

Plants affected Any plants.

Control methods
PHYSICAL Mist under leaves with water. Prune away infected leaves.

BIOCONTROLS Predatory mites that feed on two-spotted mite are commercially available for large-scale and home garden use. Do not use chemicals, even organic pesticides, where predatory mites are active. Introduce predators when plants are in active growth.

CHEMICAL Sulphur dusted under leaves can reduce numbers. Eco-oil and neem are registered for use against mites but will also kill predators. Systemic insecticides registered for mites are not suited to organic gardening.

BELOW This leaf has been damaged by plague thrips. Thrips often feed in flowers and, as well, can affect fruit set and reduce crops. They are often worse in dry and windy conditions.

BELOW An infestation of two-spotted mite, also known as red spider mite.

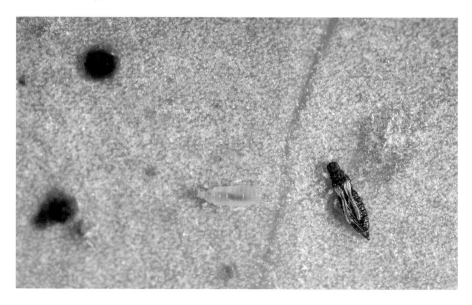

Comment

There are many other mites that affect both productive and ornamental plants. Many are so tiny they can't be seen even with a magnifying glass. Some mites may affect early growth and flower buds, causing distortions and fruit drop.

WHITEFLY

These tiny white-winged insects suck sap from plants and fly up in a cloud when they are disturbed.

Active season Any time, but most prevalent in late spring and summer when plants are actively growing.

Plants affected Many plants, but particularly tomatoes and mint.

Control methods

PHYSICAL Water affected plants thoroughly to counteract moisture loss through feeding. Sticky yellow traps (available from organic suppliers) hung near affected plants can reduce numbers. The yellow colour attracts pest insects that are then trapped by the sticky covering much like old-fashioned flypaper. These traps can also catch beneficial insects and even small birds so don't use where there are small birds or large numbers of beneficial insects.

BIOCONTROLS None commercially available.

CHEMICAL Whiteflies are resistant to many chemicals and they can be hard to contact with organic sprays. Systemic insecticides registered for whiteflies are not suited to organic gardening.

Comment

Extra watering during times of whitefly attack can help reduce damage to plants.

ABOVE Whitefly can be present on leafy plants in large numbers especially during summer when crops are actively growing. Sticky traps can reduce their numbers as part of an organic approach to their control.

OTHER PROBLEMS

Plants can be adversely affected by many physical factors including drought, over-watering, temperature extremes, frost, hail and over-fertilising. Limit the effect of these problems by growing plants that are adapted to the climatic conditions in your area, by protecting them from extremes of hot and cold, and applying appropriate amounts of water and fertiliser. Poorly grown plants or damage during planting can also lead to problems with growth and development.

Physical condition	Plant problem
drought	wilting, dieback, dead or damaged leaves, poor flowering, fruit drop, stunted growth, plant death
frost	burnt appearance, blackened growth, dieback, plant death after cold or frosty weather
hail	leaf spotting, pitting of leaves and stems, split bark, dieback of tips or entire branches after a hail storm
heat	burnt leaves, dieback; damage often occurs on the western side of the plant
lightning strike	splitting of trunks, often in a spiral pattern; death of tall or solitary tree
over-watering	yellow leaves, wilting growth, dieback
root-bound plants	stunting, susceptible to disease, water stress
soil compaction	dieback, plant death
transplant shock	dieback or sudden death of new plantings
under-watering	yellowing leaves, wilting, plant death

Diseases

BLOSSOM END ROT

Blossom end rot is a disorder of some fruit caused by a lack of calcium and exacerbated by erratic watering. Tomatoes form brown leathery patches on the base, where the flower was attached.

Active season Summer, while fruit is forming.

Plants affected Tomato, capsicum, pumpkin, zucchini and squash.

Control methods
PHYSICAL Regular watering while fruit is forming. Remove affected fruit.

BIOCONTROLS None.

CHEMICAL Add calcium at planting.

Comment
This disorder can be confused with incomplete fertilisation, which causes female pumpkin and zucchini flowers to fall without setting fruit.

DAMPING OFF

This is a disease of seedlings that causes them to die, often by rotting or becoming weakened at soil level. Seedlings may appear to have fallen over. Germinating seeds can also be affected. It is caused by soil-borne pathogens such as rhizoctonia, pythium and phytophthora, along with botrytis, which causes grey mould.

Active season Any time, but often in spring and summer during wet or humid conditions.

Plants affected All seedlings.

Control methods
PHYSICAL Start off seeds or seedlings in seed trays, punnets or individual pots. Make sure soil is well drained when seedlings are transplanted and thin the seedlings to avoid overcrowding. Plant healthy seedlings in an area not previously affected by damping off.

BIOCONTROLS Digging compost into affected areas may boost helpful microorganisms in the soil.

CHEMICAL Drench soil and seedlings at planting with a fungicide solution. Organic gardeners may apply phosphorous acid, tea tree oil or homemade fungicide (see Chapter 12, page 183 for recipes).

Comment
Seedlings that appear to have been cut off at ground level may also be affected by cutworm, which is a caterpillar.

GREY MOULD

Also known as botrytis, grey mould affects fruit and flowers (and can also cause damping off of seedlings, as discussed above). Flowers become brown or may develop spots and discolouration. As this fungal disease progresses it may develop white or grey furry growth (fungal hyphae) and affected flowers and fruit can rot. Premature loss of flowers can affect fruit formation and reduce crop yields.

Active season Can occur throughout the year but usually worse in warm, humid periods or after rain.

Plants affected Many plants, but particularly grapes and roses.

Control methods
PHYSICAL Remove affected fruit and flowers. Prune and remove weeds to increase air circulation.

BIOCONTROLS Not applicable.

CHEMICAL Apply a registered organic fungicide.

Comment
Botrytis in ripe grapes (known as 'noble rot') can give wines the sweet flavour favoured in dessert wines.

LEAF SPOTTING

A large range of disease problems can cause leaf spotting, including fungal diseases and a number of viral problems. Leaves that are burnt or damaged by wind, or which may also have been damaged by heat, frost or hail, may develop secondary fungal problems. Over-fertilising and nutrient deficiencies can also lead to damage that resembles leaf spotting.

Active season Any time, but more common when it is hot, wet or humid.

Plants affected Many plants.

Control methods
PHYSICAL Remove damaged leaves and increase air circulation around plants. Avoid watering foliage. Water and feed plants to encourage new growth.

BIOCONTROLS Not applicable.

CHEMICAL Treat persistent problems with a suitable registered fungicide. Winter sprays and washes using copper or sulphur can reduce some leaf spotting problems in deciduous plants.

Comment
Check the underside of leaf spots for any sign of pest damage. Spots on the upper sides of leaves that are not caused by fungal problems may also be the result of insects feeding. Where leaf spotting is seen always check for the presence of pests such as scale, thrips or two-spotted mite.

ABOVE Leaf spotting occurs on a range of plants. It may be a fungal disease or be caused by physical conditions, nutrient deficiencies or even pests.

ABOVE Powdery mildew can disfigure and distort foliage, for example on grapevines, and also affects flower buds.

POWDERY MILDEW

A white, powdery dusting over the top side of leaves indicates powdery mildew. As the disease progresses, leaves may brown and die. The disease also affects buds and flowers.

Active season Any season but often in cool, humid weather.

Plants affected Many plants, but particularly cucurbits, including zucchini, pumpkin and cucumber. Also roses and hydrangeas.

Control methods

PHYSICAL Remove affected leaves. Where infestation is severe remove plants. Pick up discarded leaves. Remove weeds and improve air circulation around plants. Avoid wetting foliage. Practise crop rotation.

BIOCONTROLS Not applicable.

CHEMICAL Use a registered fungicide such as potassium bicarbonate, sulphur or copper. Homemade preventative solutions based on bicarbonate of soda or milk may prevent or slow the appearance of this disease. See page 183 for recipes.

Comment

Add a wetting agent or a fungal soap product to fungicides to ensure the product adheres to the leaf surface. Grow mildew-resistant varieties.

ROOT ROT DISEASES

As well as causing damping off in seedlings (see page 174), soil-borne fungi such as phytophthora, pythium and rhizoctonia can damage or kill larger plants including trees, shrubs and perennials. Phytophthora is referred to as jarrah dieback and is responsible for the death of Australian native forests in Western Australia. Crown rot affects some perennial plants. The causal fungi are often spread through the soil by water but can also be carried to fresh areas on feet and tools.

Active season Any time, but often becomes obvious in wet or poorly drained soils.

Plants affected Most (although some plants show resistance to some root rot fungi).

Control methods
PHYSICAL Remove affected plants. Increase hygiene methods, including avoiding moving soil from one area to another. Sterilise garden tools and shoes. Avoid bringing soil or plant material from other areas where root rot may be a problem. Avoid over-wetting the soil and allow to dry out between watering. If using recycled or dam water, check the water as it can be a source of contamination. Don't allow mulch to build up around stems, crowns or trunks.

BIOCONTROLS Look for resistant varieties or plants grafted onto root rot-resistant understock (for more on understock see page 48). Compost can assist the build-up of beneficial soil microorganisms.

CHEMICAL Apply a fungal soil drench such as phosphorous acid where root rot is suspected, treating affected as well as unaffected plants.

Comment
This is a severe disease that can be very hard to control.

RUST

The disease known as rust covers many fungal problems but all are characterised by orange or brown rusty pustules on leaves. Severe infestations can lead to leaf drop and may weaken plants.

Active season Any time, but mainly warm, humid periods.

Plants affected Many, but particularly ornamental plants including rose, hollyhock, snapdragon, fuchsia and geranium. Also found on mint, onion and rhubarb. Myrtle rust affects plants in the Myrtaceae family including lillypillies.

Control methods
PHYSICAL Remove affected leaves. Where infestation is severe remove plants. Pick up discarded leaves. Remove weeds and improve air circulation around plants. Avoid wetting foliage. Grow resistant varieties if available. Practise crop rotation.

BIOCONTROLS Not applicable.

CHEMICAL Use a registered fungicide such as potassium bicarbonate, sulphur or copper. Homemade solutions based on bicarbonate of soda or milk may prevent or slow the appearance of this disease.

Comment
This disease can spread rapidly so remove infected leaves quickly and dispose of safely.

SCAB

A fungal disease that affects many fruit trees, causing brown patches on leaves, fruit and stems.

Active season Any time but particularly in mild, damp conditions.

Plants affected Many, but particularly fruit trees such as apple and pear.

ABOVE Rust is found on the leaves of many edible and ornamental plants.

Control methods
PHYSICAL Remove affected fruit and branches. Rake up fallen leaves. Grow resistant varieties if available. Prune to encourage good air flow by creating open-centred trees.

BIOCONTROLS Not applicable.

CHEMICAL Apply copper, lime or sulphur sprays in winter.

Comments
Scab can affect fruit yield as flowers are lost. This disease can also affect stored fruit.

SOOTY MOULD

This black growth that can cover the surfaces of leaves and stems is a secondary infection. It grows on the honeydew exuded by aphids or scale feeding on the plant. To remove the mould, deal with the pest problem.

Active season Any time, but more likely when pests are active.

Plants affected Many. May also affect neighbouring plants.

Control methods
PHYSICAL Remove pest by pruning (see pages 165 and 170 for control methods for sap-sucking pests including aphids and scale).

BIOCONTROLS Not applicable.

CHEMICAL A soap spray or hosing will remove the black residue once the pest has been dealt with.

Comment
Sooty mould and ants are an indication of pest problems and plant stress.

VIRUS

There are many viruses that can affect plants. They are often spread by insects such as aphids. Damage can include discolouration of foliage, restricted growth and plant death. Specific viruses affecting fruit and vegetables include tomato wilt virus, big bud, mosaic virus and woodiness of passionfruit.

Active season Any time, but more likely when pests are active.

Plants affected Many.

Control methods
PHYSICAL Remove affected plants. To limit spread, also remove weeds and control sap-sucking pests. Sterilise pruning tools. Buy certified virus-free plants such as strawberries and potatoes.

BIOCONTROLS Not applicable.

CHEMICAL There are no chemical controls for viral infections.

Comment
Good hygiene and attention to pests can reduce viral problems.

Deficiencies

A lack of macro- or micro-nutrients can affect plant growth (stunting), leaf colour, flowering and fruiting. Deficiencies may show up as specific patterns on foliage, but these may vary from plant to plant. Often older leaves are affected. Pale green leaves may indicate nitrogen deficiency; yellow or reddish leaf edges may indicate potassium deficiency; pale yellow leaves may indicate phosphorus deficiency. Problems such as cankers or discolouration of fruit may be a boron deficiency. Calcium deficiency also affects fruiting (see blossom end rot page 174).

Active season Any time but often more apparent when plants are actively growing.

Plants affected All, but often obvious in citrus trees.

Control methods
PHYSICAL Check soil pH. Extremely acid or alkaline soils can reduce the availability of soil nutrients (see page 103 for details on how to test soil pH). Grow affected plants in raised beds or containers with potting mix. Use rainwater if tap water is highly alkaline.

BIOCONTROL Not applicable.

CHEMICAL Adjust soil pH. Add extra nutrients. Add lime at planting if soil is alkaline.

Comment
If soil conditions in your area are extremely alkaline or acidic, select plants that are naturally adapted to those conditions.

IRON DEFICIENCY

When the pH of the soil is alkaline (a pH of 7 or above) acid-loving plants such as citrus and gardenia are unable to tap into vital soil nutrients such as iron. One result of a lack of iron is lime-induced chlorosis. Affected plants develop yellow leaves with prominent green veins. Correct with iron chelates. Mix iron chelates in water following the instructions on the container and apply it as a leaf spray and to soil around the root area. Leaves should begin to green up in five to seven days (reaction time is slower in cold weather). Repeat the application every two to four weeks.

Note: For long-term correction, apply sulphur to the soil to lower its pH. Retest the soil regularly and adjust as necessary.

CHAPTER 12

Organic recipes for pest and disease control

Why do I need to read this chapter?

Organic tips and treatments

As well as reaching for a chemically based treatment for garden problems you may encounter with your plants, it is handy to have some physical aids as well. These take the form of some type of material to provide temporary cover against sun, frost and wind along with materials to repair damaged plants.

Many plants can be encouraged to help themselves fight back against pest or diseases if they are growing strongly. Healthy plants contain starches which provide energy allowing the plant to withstand tough times.

To help plants stay healthy, keep the soil well nourished to encourage lots of beneficial organisms to live in and around plant roots. Compost, rotted manure and mulch help soil organisms to thrive as does seaweed, which can be applied as a liquid or, if available, as mulch.

Plants are also vulnerable to pests and diseases if they become water stressed. Take care to keep all plants (both productive and ornamental) well watered to avoid pests and disease problems.

To be ready to help your plants, make sure these items are handy. For a help list, see 'First aid box for plants', opposite.

Which method?

Many suitable pre-packaged organic pesticide products for the control of both pests and diseases are now available. The benefits of ready-made products bought off the shelf include consistency, product registration and recommended control rates on the label to avoid damage to plants and non-target insects.

However, a host of homemade remedies can be prepared as needed using simple household ingredients. The benefits of these homemade remedies are that they are usually cheap, benign and can be made up in the quantities that are needed to avoid waste.

Off-the-shelf products available to organic gardeners include those based on oils, postassium soap and *Bacillus thuringiensis*, as well as plant extracts such as quassia, neem and pyrethrum.

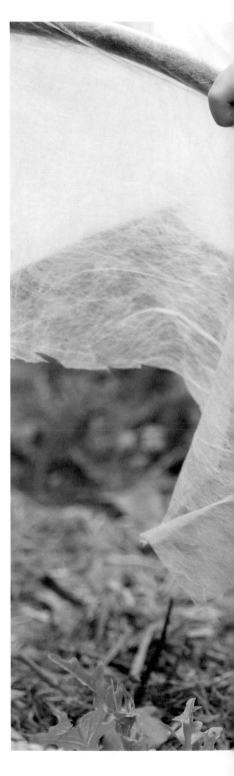

Tip In very hot summer regions or where you have made new plantings of permanent plants, erect a simple, portable frame using recycled timber and shadecloth to make the task of shading plants easier to manage.

LEFT Horticultural fleece attached to hoops made from irrigation pipe can be used to protect early plantings from frost. In hot areas use shadecloth to protect from sun scorch.

First aid box for plants

Have these products handy to deal with problems you discover in the garden.

Budding or grafting tape A stretchable tape that can be used to bind up or splint broken plants or to hold buds and grafts in place.

Seaweed solution Seaweed encourages plants to heal themselves by strengthening cell walls and stimulating 'good' organisms in the soil.

Shadecloth Use a piece of shadecloth as a temporary measure to protect vulnerable plants on hot days from the heat of the sun. Instant shade reduces water stress, crop damage and leaf scald. If you don't have shadecloth, use an outdoor umbrella, hessian or cardboard.

Aged organic matter Well-rotted compost or manure can be used to encourage beneficial microorganisms in soils and to keep roots cool. Dissolved in water, it can also be used as a compost tea to feed to plants.

Phosphorous acid Sold under various brand names, this helps treat fungal problems including root rot disease. Water over the roots or foliage, heavily diluted (5–10 ml/L water).

Weed control

Herbicides are substances used to control and kill weeds. Herbicides that are commercially manufactured can be either selective or non-selective. That is there are some products that target specific types of weeds (selective) and others that kill or damage any type of plant growth (non-selective).

Most homemade herbicides are not selective—this means they'll damage any plant material they contact. Apply any herbicide with care and avoid contacting non-weedy plants including lawn grass.

SALT AND VINEGAR HERBICIDES

Salt (sodium chloride) and vinegar are readily available and the main ingredients for homemade herbicides. Salt and vinegar are non-selective weedicides.

Salt and vinegar spray

1 cup salt
1 litre vinegar
Add salt to vinegar. Stir to dissolve. Brush or spray onto weeds. Repeat as necessary.

Brown vinegar spray

brown vinegar
water
Mix 1 part brown vinegar and 1 part water. Paint or spray onto weeds. Use to control creeping oxalis in lawns (test a small section of lawn grass before applying to large areas). This spray does not work on bulbous oxalis or other persistent weeds.
Note: Keep herbicides, even organic-based products in separate container and well labelled.

Safe use of homemade sprays

Even remedies based on commonly available foods and products you may have in your pantry cupboard can affect you and your plants so take some precautions when following any of these recipes.

Check for phytotoxicity Apply homemade sprays and remedies to a test area first before spraying an entire plant or garden. It may take 24 hours for foliage damage to appear.

Safety first Keep these products out of the reach of children and pets. Do not store them in soft-drink or other containers. Always mark contents clearly.

Pollution Avoid tipping oil-based sprays down drains.

Cleanliness Wash hands thoroughly before eating. Chilli, onion and garlic sprays can irritate eyes and skin and should be handled with care.

BELOW Home-made weed control sprays may not control all weeds. Combine physical and organically acceptable chemical methods for best control.

Disease control

Bicarbonate of soda and milk, which are common household products, along with lime and copper both long used by organic gardeners, are the main ingredients used to concoct homemade fungicides to control plant diseases.

Combine chemical controls with good cultural practices including removing the affected plant parts to control diseases.

BICARBONATE-BASED FUNGICIDES

Bicarbonate, also called baking soda or bicarbonate of soda, is made from sodium carbonate. Buy it in bulk to reduce costs.

Bicarbonate of soda spray

This fungicide spray helps prevent black spot and powdery mildew. Apply frequently to susceptible plants such as roses and grapevines.

3 teaspoons bicarbonate of soda
1 litre water
fish emulsion (or dishwashing liquid)

Mix bicarbonate of soda in water. Add a few drops of either fish emulsion or dishwashing liquid to allow the solution to adhere to the leaf more effectively.

General fungicide

This is an all-purpose fungicide mix.
1 teaspoon bicarbonate of soda
1 litre water
1 litre milk (full cream)
Condy's crystals (potassium permanganate)

Mix bicarbonate of soda in water. Add milk and a pinch of Condy's crystals. Shake thoroughly and spray as needed. Note: Condy's crystals are available from produce stores, feed supply stores and some chemists.

COPPER-BASED FUNGICIDES

Copper is a naturally occurring element that can be used in a plant spray to prevent or kill many types of disease organisms such as brown rot. Copper-based sprays are particularly useful as winter sprays when deciduous plants are bare.

Care should be taken in applying these sprays as they can kill earthworms in the soil. Try to restrict overspray and run-off to reduce the amount that soaks into the soil. A layer of mulch can also reduce the impact of copper spray on the soil.

Copper is available as Bordeaux mixture (see the following recipe to make your own), as copper sulphate and copper oxychloride, and in the preparation sold as Fungus Fighter. Mix and apply copper-based fungicides according to the instructions on the container.

Bordeaux mix

This mix contains copper and lime. It is used to control fungal diseases. Apply to bare bark and deciduous plants in winter.
1 cup copper sulphate
10 litres water
1 dessertspoon lime

Stir ingredients together and spray or paint onto the bark of trees. Avoid contact with foliage.

LIME-BASED PEST AND DISEASE CONTROL

Lime sprays are effective against a wide range of diseases and can also control pests including scale insects. They are best applied to bark and to dormant plants.

Lime sprays include lime sulphate and Bordeaux mixture (recipe above). Don't mix lime sprays with oils. Don't apply to plants within three weeks of applying an oil spray.

MILK-BASED FUNGICIDES

Milk is an effective fungicidal agent. The fat in milk helps it work, so use full-cream milk. Powdered milk can be used.

Milk works by changing the pH of the of the surface of the foliage on which it is sprayed to render it less hospitable to organisms such as fungus spore.

Apply milk as a preventative spray to reduce the likelihood of fungal attack. Apply milk diluted with water in a ratio of 1 part milk to 5 parts water. Repeat this preventative spray frequently and reapply after rain.

Pest control

Make up some of the following recipes to kill pests on plants or to keep them at bay. Follow the instructions for their use to avoid phytotoxicity (burning or discolouration triggered by chemicals). Always test a homemade spray on a small part of the plant before spraying it all over.

CHILLI- AND GARLIC-BASED PEST CONTROLS

Chilli spray

Capsaicin, which makes chillies hot to our palate, can deter some insects and animals from eating your crops. Birds do not appear to be sensitive to capsaicin so chilli sprays are not effective in deterring them.

4 large onions
2 garlic cloves
4 hot chillies
1 litre warm water
a few drops of detergent
*   or 1 teaspoon of soap flakes*

Chop onions, garlic and chillies. Mix them together and cover with warm soapy water. Leave to steep overnight. Strain off the liquid. Dilute the strained liquid in 5 litres of water and spray on insects.

Garlic spray

50 g garlic, crushed
150 ml liquid paraffin (to cover garlic)
2.5 litres water
150 g pure soap (e.g. flakes or grated)

Soak garlic in paraffin for 24–48 hours. Stir in water and soap. Strain to remove garlic solids then store in glass bottles. Keep out of direct sun. To use, dilute 1 part garlic mix with 3 parts water. Use against snails and caterpillars.

COFFEE-BASED PEST CONTROLS

Caffeine has gained a higher profile in organic gardens in recent years as it is an excellent deterrent against soft-bodied snails and slugs. A 1–2 per cent solution of caffeine can kill these pests. Take care when applying coffee to plants as it can damage some foliage.

Caffeine spray

Caffeine is toxic to snails and slugs. Use a ring of coffee grounds around seedlings as a snail and slug deterrent or make this spray to protect plants.

1 part strong espresso coffee
10 parts water

Mix and spray liberally on the foliage and soil around plants that are vulnerable to snails or slugs.

PEST CONTROLS USING OTHER INGREDIENTS

Molasses spray

Molasses is used to control nematodes (also called eelworms) in soil.

molasses
water

Mix 1 part molasses to 4 parts water. Apply to soil. As a guide, 2 litres of water covers 1.5 square metres of garden bed.

Nettle spray

Weedy stinging nettle (*Urtica* spp.) can be transformed into a general-purpose insect spray that's especially effective in controlling aphids.

1 bucket of young nettles
water to cover

Steep the nettles for 5 to 7 days, strain, and spray on garden pests such as aphids. Nettles can also be thrown into compost heaps as an activator or steeped in water (as above) to form a liquid fertiliser called nettle tea.

Warning Wear gloves when harvesting nettles as they sting.

Oil-based spray

2 cups vegetable oil
½ cup liquid soap

Mix oil and soap in a blender. Dilute 1 tablespoon of the oil mix in 1 litre water. Spray on mites and scale.

Tip Do not apply on hot days.

RIGHT Snails are devastating in gardens and can be present in very large numbers. They are particularly damaging to new seedlings but also damage foliage. They are often active at night and especially after rain or heavy watering. In addition to baits, barriers and sprays also physically remove snails by hunting them at night.

CHAPTER 13

Further reading and supplier information

This reading list is divided into topics and further divided into details for useful magazines, books and websites. Some of the books are no longer in print so they must be sourced from second-hand book suppliers or from libraries.

Permaculture

Books

Jenny Allen, *Paradise in Your Garden: Smart Permaculture Design*, New Holland Publishers, Sydney, 2002.

David Holmgren, *Permaculture: Principles and Pathways Beyond Sustainability*, Holmgren Design Services, Hepburn, Victoria, 2002.

Bill Mollison, *Permaculture: A Designers' Manual*, Tagari Press, Sisters Creek, Tasmania, 1988. This is the seminal book about the theory of permaculture, written by the founder of the permaculture movement.

Bill Mollison, *Permaculture Two*, Tagari Press, Sisters Creek, Tasmania, 1979.

Bill Mollison & David Holmgren, *Permaculture One*, Transworld Publishers, Melbourne, 1978.

Bill Mollison & Reny Mia Slay, *Introduction to Permaculture*, Tagari Press, Sisters Creek, Tasmania, 1997.

Rosemary Morrow, *Earth User's Guide to Permaculture*, Kangaroo Press, Sydney, 1993; 2nd edn, Simon & Schuster, Sydney, 2007.

Linda Woodrow, *The Permaculture Home Garden*, Penguin Group, Melbourne, 2007.

Websites

David Holmgren:
http://www.holmgren.com.au

Milkwood Permaculture:
www.milkwoodpermaculture.com.au

Listings of Bill Mollison's texts and courses:
www.tagari.com

Permaculture College Australia:
http://permaculture.com.au/online/index.php

The Permaculture Research Institute of Australia:
http://permaculture.org.au

Permaforest Trust:
www.permaforesttrust.org.au

Biodynamic

Books

Manfred Klett, *Principles of Biodynamic Spray and Compost Preparation*, Floris Books, Edinburgh, 2005.

Rudolf Steiner, *What is Biodynamics? A Way to Heal and Revitalize the Earth*, SteinerBooks Inc., Dulles, VA, 2007.

Maria Thun, *The Biodynamic Year*, Temple Lodge Publishing, Forest Row, East Sussex, 2007.

Hilary Wright, *Biodynamic Gardening: For Health and Taste*, Floris Books, Edinburgh, 2009.

Websites

Biodynamic Agriculture Australia:
www.biodynamics.net.au

Biodynamics2024:
biodynamics2024.com.au

Organic gardening and sustainable practices

Magazines

ABC *Gardening Australia* magazine
www.gardeningaustralia.com.au
Phone: (02) 8062 2918 (editorial);
1300 656 933 (subscriptions)
Email: ga@newsmagazines.com.au

Organic Gardener
www.organicgardener.com.au
Phone: (02) 6688 6348 (editorial);
(03) 8317 8110 (subscriptions, back issues)
Email: hummingwords@internode.on.net

General reference books

Lyn Bagnall *Easy Organic Gardening and Moon Planting*,
Scribe Publications, Melbourne, 2006.

Clive Blazey & Jane Varkulevicius, *Australian Fruit & Vegetable
Growing*, The Digger's Club, Dromana, Victoria, 2008.

Josh Byrne, *The Green Gardener*, Penguin Viking, Melbourne,
2006.

Monty Don, *The Organic Gardener*, Dorling Kindersley,
London, 2006.

Geoff Hamilton, *Successful Organic Gardening*, Murdoch
Books, London, 1987.

Kevin Handreck & Neil Black, *Growing Media for Ornamental
Plants and Turf*, 4th edn, UNSW Press, Sydney, 2010.

Jeffrey Hodges, *Natural Gardening in Australia*, 2nd edn, Viking,
Melbourne, 2002.

Erin Hynes, *Rodale's Successful Organic Gardening: Improving the
Soil*, Rodale Press, Emmaus, PA, 1994.

Brenda Little, *The Australian Organic Gardening Handbook*,
Sandstone Publishing, Sydney, 2000.

Annette McFarlane, *Organic Fruit Growing*, ABC Books/
HarperCollins, Sydney, 2011.

Annette McFarlane, *Organic Vegetable Gardening*, ABC Books/
HarperCollins, Sydney, 2010.

General websites

Alternative Technology Association website for information
on greywater system options, hygiene and environmental
issues and rebates: www.ata.org.au/sustainability/
greywater-systems

Brisbane organic growers: www.bogi.org.au

Department of Agriculture and Food, Western Australia: For
a series of excellent downloadable leaflets on pests, diseases
and pruning, see: www.agric.wa.gov.au/objtwr/imported_
assets/content/hort/fn/cp/pruning.pdf

Eco Organic Garden is the website of Organic Crop
Protectants, a company that produces organic certified
garden products including fruit fly lures, neem and organic
fungicides. For more information see:
www.ecoorganicgarden.com.au

Edible Gardens: www.edible-gardens.info

Green businesses: www.thegreendirectory.com.au

For numerous links to organic gardening resources:
www.greenharvest.com.au

Lanfax Laboratories for independent research on the
suitability of detergents for greywater re-use: www.
lanfaxlabs.com.au

Organic gardening groups and associations

Australian Certified Organic

This organisation licenses growers and suppliers to use their Australian Certified Organic symbol. A list of certified suppliers of organic products can also be found on the website. Also see Biological Farmers of Australia (BFA), right.

www.aco.net.au
Phone: (07) 3350 5716
Fax: (07) 3350 5996
Email: info@bfa.com.au
Mail: PO Box 530, Chermside Qld 4032

The Bio-Dynamic Gardeners Association Inc. (BDGAI)

Advisory organisation for home gardeners and hobby farmers.

www.demeter.org.au
Phone: (03) 9842 8137
Fax: n/a
Email: n/a
Mail: 4A Fairleigh Ave, Beaumaris VIC 3193

Bio-Dynamic Gardening & Farming Association in Australia (BDGFAA)

www.biodynamics.net.au
Phone: (02) 6655 8551
Fax: (02) 6655 8551
Email: bdoffice@biodynamics.net.au
Mail: PO Box 54, Bellingen NSW 2454

Biological Farmers of Australia (BFA)

Provides certification for organic producers.

www.bfa.com.au
Phone: (07) 3350 5716
Fax: (07) 3350 5996
Email: info@bfa.com.au
Mail: PO Box 530, Chermside QLD 4032

Demeter Bio-Dynamic Research Institute

Books, videos and DVDs about biodynamics available from the Bio-Dynamic Marketing Co. Ltd.

www.demeter.org.au
Phone: (03) 5966 7333
Fax: (03) 5966 7339
Email: n/a
Mail: Main Rd, Powelltown VIC 3797

NASAA

Provides certification for organic produce.

www.nasaa.com.au
Phone: (08) 8370 8455
Fax: (08) 8370 8381
Email: enquiries@nasaa.com.au
Mail: PO Box 768, Stirling SA 5152

Sustainable Gardening Australia (SGA)

www.sgaonline.org.au
Phone: (03) 9850 8165
Fax: (03) 9852 1097
Email: vic@sgaonline.org.au
Mail: 6 Manningham Road West Bulleen, Vic 3105

Suppliers of organic products including seeds

These companies have organic products including seeds, crop protection materials, organic pesticides and some also stock a range of useful books.

The Digger's Club

The Digger's Club offers discount to club members and produces regular newsletters and catalogues.
www.diggers.com.au
Phone: (03) 5984 7900
Fax: (03) 5987 2398
Email: info@diggers.com.au
Mail: PO Box 300, Dromana VIC 3936

Eden Seeds

As well as providing a list of their products, the Eden Seeds website provides a comprehensive list of other suppliers and organic organisations.
www.edenseeds.com.au
Phone: (07) 5533 1107
Fax: (07) 5533 1108
Email: n/a; to order products visit www.selectorganic.com.au (click on 'Browse Seeds')
Mail: Eden Seeds, MS 905, Lower Beechmont QLD 4211

Fruit Spirit Botanical Garden

www.nrg.com.au/~recher
Phone: (02) 6689 5192
Fax: n/a
Email: recher@nrg.com.au
Mail: Lot 69 Dunoon Rd, Dorroughby NSW 2480

Green Harvest

Green Harvest has a printed catalogue available.
www.greenharvest.com.au
Phone: (07) 5435 2699; 1800 681 014 (orders only)
Fax: n/a
Email: inquiries@greenharvest.com.au
Mail: Box 92, Maleny QLD 4552

Greenpatch Organic Seeds

Open-pollinated, non-hybrid and organic seed supplier.
www.greenpatchseeds.com.au
Phone: (02) 6551 4240
Fax: (02) 6551 4240
Email: enquiries@greenpatchseeds.com.au
Mail: PO Box 1285, Taree NSW 2430

The Lost Seed

For rare, open-pollinated, heritage and heirloom vegetable and herb seed varieties.
www.thelostseed.com.au
Phone: (03) 6491 1000
Fax: (03) 6491 1010
Email: mail@thelostseed.com.au
Mail: PO Box 321, Sheffield TAS 7306

Seed Savers Network

This international organisation is dedicated to the preservation of cultivated varieties of fruit and vegetables. You can join Seed Savers to help preserve varieties by growing them in your garden and saving seed from your crop.
www.seedsavers.net
Phone: (02) 6685 7560
Fax: (02) 6685 6624
Email: info@seedsavers.net
Mail: PO Box 975, Byron Bay NSW 2481

Fruit tree suppliers

Regular nursery-grown plants are not always raised by organic methods.

Daley's Nursery

Subtropical fruit and nut trees, forestation trees, herbs and rainforest trees.
www.daleysfruit.com.au
Phone: (02) 6632 1441
Fax: (02) 6632 2585
Email: gdaley@primus.com.au
Mail: PO Box 154, Kyogle NSW 2474

Forbidden Fruits Nursery

Complete range of citrus, fruit and nut trees.
www.forbiddenfruitsnursery.com
Phone: (02) 6684 3688
Fax: (02) 6684 3688
Email: forbiddenfruits@optusnet.com.au
Mail: 246 McAuleys Lane, Mullumbimby NSW 2482

New Zealand contacts

Biodynamic
Bio Dynamic Farming & Gardening Association
in New Zealand
http://www.biodynamic.org.nz/

Kings Seeds
www.kingsseeds.co.nz
Phone: (07) 549 3409
Fax: (07) 549 3408
Email: info@kingsseeds.co.nz
Mail: PO Box 283, Katikati 3166, Bay of Plenty, NZ
Location: 189 Wharawhara Road, RD 2, Katikati 3178

Australian and New Zealand soil labs

Contact the laboratory to check on procedures for sending soil samples for analysis.

Australian Perry Agricultural Laboratory
www.apal.com.au
Phone: (08) 8332 0199
Fax: (08) 8361 2715
Email: info@apal.com.au
Mail: 489 The Parade, Magill SA 5072 or PO Box 327, Magill SA 5072

Department of Primary Industries, NSW
http://www.dpi.nsw.gov.au/aboutus/services/das/soils

Lanfax Laboratories
www.lanfaxlabs.com.au
Phone: (02) 6775 1157
Fax: (02) 6775 1043
Email: lanfaxlabs@bigpond.com.au
Mail: PO Box 4690, Armidale NSW 2350

SWEP Analytical Laboratories
www.swep.com.au/pages/home/home.html
Phone: 030 9701 6007
Email: services@swep.com.au

Mail: PO Box 583, Noble Park VIC 3174
Delivery address or for postage from outside Australia:
Unit 47/174 Bridge Rd, Keysborough VIC 3173

Sydney Environmental & Soil Laboratory
www.sesl.com.au
Phone: (02) 9980 6554
Fax: (02) 9484 2427
Email: enter website
Mail: PO Box 357, Pennant Hills NSW 1715
Sample drop-off: 16 Chilvers Road, Thornleigh NSW 2120

Hill Laboratories (New Zealand)
www.hill-laboratories.com
Phone: (07) 858 2000 (North Island); (03) 377 7176 (South Island)

Wildlife rescue groups

Often our garden puts us in contact with injured wildlife. If you find an injured animal, pick it up using a towel and contain it in a box or safe cage. Don't attempt to feed it but do take it immediately to a vet. If you can't safely handle the animal call your local wildlife rescue service (for a rescue group near you, see www.fauna.org.au), vet, police or council for more information.

Bat Care Brisbane (07) 3321 1229

Bat Rescue Gold Coast 0447 222 889

FAWNA (NSW) 0500 861 405

Sydney Metropolitan Wildlife Services (02) 9413 4300

WIRES (NSW) 1300 094 737

Index

Picture credits

All photographs by Ian Hofstetter, except for the following:

Graphic Science 172 (left and right)

istockphoto.com 16, 57 (right), 65 (left), 67, 74 (top), 77 (bottom), 87, 108 (bottom), 117, 131, 144 (right), 147 (right), 151 (left), 158 (right), 165 (left and right), 167 (right), 169 (right), 170 (right), 171, 173, 185

Lorna Rose 10, 29–30, 34, 37 (bottom), 41 (top and bottom left), 44, 47, 49, 53, 58, 63, 116 (top), 135 (right), 140, 154 (right), 155 (left), 162, 164, 166 (left and right), 167 (left), 175, 176

Murdoch Books Photo Library 2, 15, 18, 24, 26, 28 (right), 31, 36, 39, 60, 71 (left), 97, 99 (bottom), 104 (left), 121, 142 (left), 148 (right), 149, 157 (left), 168 (left), 169 (left)

Natasha Milne 54 (bottom), 92 (right), 148 (left), 154 (left), 155 (right), 159 (right), 186

Robin Powell 42

photolibrary.com 145

Sue Stubbs 4, 46, 50, 52, 54, 57 (left), 71 (right), 80–2, 84, 89 (right), 90 (right), 91, 104 (right), 105 (right), 107 (left), 110, 112, 114, 115, 116 (middle and bottom), 120, 125 (right), 127, 130 (right), 134, 136, 138–9, 141, 142 (right), 143, 144 (left), 146, 147 (left), 150, 151 (right), 152–3, 156, 157 (right), 158 (left), 159 (left), 160–1, 168 (right), 178, 180, 182 (left), 194

About the authors

Jennifer Stackhouse's interest in horticulture and writing was inspired by her family background. After leaving university she began curatorial work at Sydney's Elizabeth Bay House museum, researching the extensive garden that once surrounded the house, and arranging exhibitions of historic plants and heritage roses; it was here that she decided to learn more about plants and gardening. After completing an Associate Diploma in Horticulture, Jennifer joined the staff of the Royal Botanic Gardens. She began her career in horticultural media soon afterwards; she currently writes regularly for *Sunday Herald Sun*, *Daily Telegraph* and *Mercury* and other newspapers around Australia and is editor of the well-respected ABC *Gardening Australia* magazine.

Jennifer has a large garden on the outskirts of Sydney, two children, numerous cats, dogs and chooks, and works as an editor, journalist and horticultural consultant.

Debbie McDonald discovered a passion for gardening and sharing the joy of gardens through writing after a short career in the fashion and textile industry. She has been horticultural editor at ABC *Gardening Australia* magazine since 2003, after working for several years as a gardener, garden designer and horticultural consultant. She also edits the magazine of the *Friends of the Botanic Gardens*, Sydney, writes a weekly gardening column in *The Manly Daily*, and loves nothing better than to garden with her young daughter.

Acknowledgements

A book like this takes lots of time to create and impinges on day to day life and particularly family time so we want to say thanks to our families for their help, support and advice while we were both hard at work on this book. So thank you to: Kiera Beauman, Margery and John Postlethwaite, Greg Prentice, Helen Stackhouse, Shirley and John Stackhouse, and Jim, Rowan and Eleanor Taylor. Where would we be with out you!

Also a 'Thanks guys!' to our colleagues on ABC *Gardening Australia* magazine: Anna, Frank, Gina, Jenny, Justin, Karen, Kate, Lili, Susan and Susan.

Jennifer and Debbie

Published in 2012 by Murdoch Books Pty Limited

Murdoch Books Australia
Pier 8/9
23 Hickson Road
Millers Point NSW 2000
Phone: +61 (0) 2 8220 2000
Fax: +61 (0) 2 8220 2558
www.murdochbooks.com.au
info@murdochbooks.com.au

Murdoch Books UK Limited
Erico House, 6th Floor
93–99 Upper Richmond Road
Putney, London SW15 2TG
Phone: +44 (0) 20 8785 5995
Fax: +44 (0) 20 8785 5985
www.murdochbooks.co.uk
info@murdochbooks.co.uk

For Corporate Orders & Custom Publishing contact Noel Hammond,
National Business Development Manager Murdoch Books Australia

Chief Executive: Matt Handbury
Publishing Director: Chris Rennie
Project Editor: Emma Hutchinson
Designer: Jacqueline Richards
Production: Joan Beal

Text and Design © Murdoch Books Pty Limited 2012
Photography © Murdoch Books Pty Limited 2012
Cover photography by Sue Stubbs

Author: Stackhouse, Jennifer.
Title: The organic guide to edible gardens / Jennifer Stackhouse and Debbie McDonald.
ISBN 978-1-74196-751-7 (pbk.)
Series: From the ground up.
Notes: Includes index.
Subjects: Organic gardening. Plants, Edible.
Other Authors/Contributors: McDonald, Debbie.
Dewey Number: 635.0484

A catalogue record for this book is available from the British Library.

Printed by 1010 Printing International Limited, China

Readers of this book must ensure that any work or project undertaken complies with local
legislative and approval requirements relevant to their particular circumstances. Furthermore,
this work is necessarily of a general nature and cannot be a substitute for appropriate
professional advice.